I0020662

Mastering Cocos2d Game Development

Master game development with Cocos2d to develop
amazing mobile games for iOS

Alex Ogorek

[PACKT] open source *
PUBLISHING   community experience distilled

BIRMINGHAM - MUMBAI

Mastering Cocos2d Game Development

Copyright © 2015 Packt Publishing

All rights reserved. No part of this book may be reproduced, stored in a retrieval system, or transmitted in any form or by any means, without the prior written permission of the publisher, except in the case of brief quotations embedded in critical articles or reviews.

Every effort has been made in the preparation of this book to ensure the accuracy of the information presented. However, the information contained in this book is sold without warranty, either express or implied. Neither the author, nor Packt Publishing, and its dealers and distributors will be held liable for any damages caused or alleged to be caused directly or indirectly by this book.

Packt Publishing has endeavored to provide trademark information about all of the companies and products mentioned in this book by the appropriate use of capitals. However, Packt Publishing cannot guarantee the accuracy of this information.

First published: April 2015

Production reference: 1210415

Published by Packt Publishing Ltd.
Livery Place
35 Livery Street
Birmingham B3 2PB, UK.

ISBN 978-1-78439-671-8

www.packtpub.com

Cover image by Alex Ogorek

Credits

Author
Alex Ogorek

Reviewers
Herin Kim
Giap Nguyen
Pranav Paharia (Game Nick: Fi.eol)
Sergio Martínez-Losa Del Rincón
Marc Estruch Tena

Commissioning Editor
Ashwin Nair

Acquisition Editors
James Jones
Greg Wild

Content Development Editor
Arwa Manasawala

Technical Editor
Madhunikita Sunil Chindarkar

Copy Editor
Vikrant Phadke

Project Coordinators
Danuta Jones
Purav Motiwalla

Proofreaders
Safis Editing
Paul Hindle
Jonathan Todd

Indexer
Priya Sane

Production Coordinator
Nitesh Thakur

Cover Work
Nitesh Thakur

About the Author

Alex Ogorek is a 4-year veteran of iOS development, who has developed everything from traditional apps to games, with over 12 apps published on Apple's App Store under the name of KeitGames (`http://www.keitgames.com/`). All of his apps and games are self-developed and published, including graphics. He has been coding since he was 16, and has loved games since he was young. Before attending USC for computer science (games) and entrepreneurship, he worked at the Cleveland Clinic Foundation as an iOS developer, working on medical iPad apps that help further research with concussions in students and athletes.

About the Reviewers

Herin Kim is a full-stack developer and a creator of HTPressableButton (https://github.com/herinkc/HTPressableButton), which was once ranked #1 on GitHub Trending for Objective-C. She was offered a full scholarship to attend an intensive Cocos2d iOS game development boot camp by a Y Combinator-backed start-up, MakeSchool, at the heart of the Cocos2d team — Apportable office. She also pitched a game that she built at the end of the boot camp on a demo day at Mountain View, California, and won the second prize in the best game awards.

Aside from building games, Herin also loves hacking projects at various Hackathons. Her first, and most favorite, Hackathon is YC Hacks, which is the first Hackathon organized by Y Combinator.

Nowadays, Herin is working on her next major mobile game using Cocos2d. You can know more about her at http://herinkim.com/ or find her on Twitter at @herinkc.

> I would like to personally thank Thanakron Tandavas for always being patient and guiding me through. He is one of the coolest and most amazing persons, partners, and developers you can find. Also, to my mother and sister: thank you for always supporting me. I am who I am today because of the three of you. I love you.

Giap Nguyen is a young and pragmatic indie game developer who is familiar with Cocos2d. He loves to make fun, addictive, and easy-to-play games for mobile devices.

Pranav Paharia (Game Nick: Fi.eol) is a game developer who works on Unity3D and Cocos2d-x technologies. He has experience of more than 2 years in game development. He has worked on a variety of aspects of game development. He is keen on gameplay and graphics programming, and has graduated in information technology.

Pranav, who is left-handed, has been fascinated by digital games since childhood, playing *Mario, Contra, Bomberman,* and so on, and luckily hailing from the first generation of gamers. He was creative in art and obsessed with solving puzzles. In his school days, he was passionate about playing competitive games. After playing for 6 years and entering college, Pranav started playing *Counter Strike* professionally. After getting his college degree from VIT University, he took the most important decision of his life — converting his passion into a profession — and hence entered the game industry. He opted for a specialized course, game programming in DSK Supinfocom, and began his endeavors in the field of game development. Seeking deep motivation in encounters with every failure and working hard on his dreams, he got the opportunity to join a small team of indie game developers. Pranav worked on *Chhota Bheem Laddoo Runner* and then on *Song of Swords,* which won the People's Choice Award in the NASSCOM Game Developer Conference 2013. After that, he worked on many more games, such as *Fish Gone Mad* and *Mario Italiano.*

While gaining experience in development, Pranav didn't make any extremity. He has experience of working with many game technologies such as RPG Maker, Construct2D, Microsoft XNA Game Studio, and SDL. He has also reviewed *Unity2D Game Development Cookbook, Packt Publishing.* He works on his own designs and prototypes in his free time. A habitual reader and writer, Pranav also writes stories and creates comic art for his games. You can always find him contemplating video game science as a highly expressive medium.

You can contact Pranav at pranavpaharia@hotmail.com.

I would like to thank my beloved Krsna for helping me know my inner passion. I would also like to thank my family for being supportive and patient in the reviewing process of this book.

Sergio Martínez-Losa Del Rincón is a computer engineer. He has loved programming languages since he was in high school, when he learned about programming and computer interaction. He always keeps learning and discovers something new to learn every day.

Sergio likes all kinds of programming languages, but he focuses his efforts on mobile development with native languages such as Objective-C (iPhone), Java (Android), and Xamarin (C#). He builds Google Glass applications when at work, as well as mobile applications for iPhone and Android devices. He also develops games for mobile devices with Cocos2d-x and Cocos2d.

Sergio likes cross-platform applications; indeed, he has reviewed *Learning Xamarin Studio*, *Packt Publishing*. He loves challenging problems and is always keen to work with new technologies. More information about his experience and details can be found at www.linkedin.com/in/sergiomtzlosa.

Marc Estruch Tena received his BS degree in multimedia engineering with honors from La Salle's Ramon Llull University, Barcelona, Spain, in 2012. Since then, he has been a research associate at the Human Sensing Laboratory in the Robotics Institute of Carnegie Mellon University, Pittsburgh, Pennsylvania, USA.

As a member of this research laboratory, Marc has developed several applications and games for web and mobile platforms using computer vision algorithms that feature the IntraFace (http://humansensing.cs.cmu.edu/intraface) software for facial image analysis. His interest in human computer interaction and his programming and design skills have led him to pursue new ways of user interaction, using different tools and frameworks.

www.PacktPub.com

Support files, eBooks, discount offers, and more

For support files and downloads related to your book, please visit www.PacktPub.com.

Did you know that Packt offers eBook versions of every book published, with PDF and ePub files available? You can upgrade to the eBook version at www.PacktPub.com and as a print book customer, you are entitled to a discount on the eBook copy. Get in touch with us at service@packtpub.com for more details.

At www.PacktPub.com, you can also read a collection of free technical articles, sign up for a range of free newsletters and receive exclusive discounts and offers on Packt books and eBooks.

https://www2.packtpub.com/books/subscription/packtlib

Do you need instant solutions to your IT questions? PacktLib is Packt's online digital book library. Here, you can search, access, and read Packt's entire library of books.

Why subscribe?

- Fully searchable across every book published by Packt
- Copy and paste, print, and bookmark content
- On demand and accessible via a web browser

Free access for Packt account holders

If you have an account with Packt at www.PacktPub.com, you can use this to access PacktLib today and view 9 entirely free books. Simply use your login credentials for immediate access.

Table of Contents

Preface

If you've ever wanted to know what goes on in a great game from start to finish, this book will guide you through that process. You will discover that your games are just a few steps away from becoming the best games possible.

You'll be guided through a project and see what makes a game stand out when hundreds, or even thousands, of similar games fail to make any lasting impact. You'll experience the simplicity of Cocos2d, Chipmunk, OALSimpleAudio, and much more. You'll be given code for some unique game mechanics that will make your game stand out from the masses. This book ensures that no matter what scale of game you're working on is — whether it is indie or for a large publisher — you'll get the skills you need to create a highly polished and enjoyable experience for your players.

What this book covers

Chapter 1, Refreshing Your Cocos2d Knowledge, describes some tools you can use when developing your Cocos2d game, how to create an Apple Developer account, and also the importance of setting flexible goals when designing your project.

Chapter 2, Failing Faster with Prototypes, talks about the need for fast iterations and getting things up and running quickly. This chapter sets up the initial outline, or wireframe, for the book's project and goes into detail about using some of the tools introduced in the first chapter.

Chapter 3, Focusing on Physics, introduces the Chipmunk physics engine and the power behind it with only a few lines of code. This chapter shows you how you can integrate touch controls, physics, and the accelerometer all within a single project with ease.

Chapter 4, Sound and Music, covers the addition of sound and music, which are integral to a gaming experience. This chapter explains how to best use OALSimpleAudio and the various ways you can use sound within your game.

Chapter 5, Creating Cool Content, shows the use of particle effects, Bézier curves, and parallax scrolling. This chapter has three mini projects as well as some additions to this book's main project.

Chapter 6, Tidying Up and Polishing, explains the important process of polishing your game. There are many topics in this chapter, ranging from button animations to graphical changes. It explains in depth what you can do to make your game progress from a concept to a finished product.

Chapter 7, Reaching Our Destination, finalizes the book's project and prepares everything for launch, including the creation of the app on iTunes Connect, setting up the loading screen and app icon, and adding analytics. This chapter also covers how to actually submit the game to the App Store and what to do after you submit it.

Chapter 8, Exploring Swift, introduces the Swift programming language (and the use of Swift with Cocos2d) through the creation of a very simple game. This chapter also explains the basics of how Swift works and the main differences between Swift and Objective-C.

Chapter 9, Simple Swift App, covers the basics of creating a nongame app using Swift as the main language. Although this chapter is not available in the book, it is available for download at `https://www.packtpub.com/sites/default/files/downloads/6718OS_Chapter9.pdf`.

What you need for this book

Before reading this book, you should be armed with an understanding of how Cocos2d and Objective-C work. There is a brief introduction to Cocos2d concepts early on, but it wraps up quickly.

Besides that, anything used within the book is accompanied by a proper explanation on how to get it—whether that means downloading and installing a tool, setting up an account on iTunes Connect, or using the assets provided with this book.

Who this book is for

This book is aimed at developers who have a good handle on Cocos2d and Objective-C and want to take their game development skills to the next level. Maybe you've made games in the past that didn't get many downloads, and you want to create a higher-quality game. This book will help you polish your game to achieve what it deserves.

Conventions

In this book, you will find a number of text styles that distinguish between different kinds of information. Here are some examples of these styles and an explanation of their meaning.

Code words in text, database table names, folder names, filenames, file extensions, pathnames, dummy URLs, user input, and Twitter handles are shown as follows: "If you do not see the .xcodepoj file extension, don't worry. It should be labelled as the Xcode project in the kind filter and have a blueprint icon next to it."

A block of code is set as follows:

```
@interface MainScene : CCNode
{
  CGSize winSize;
}
+(CCScene*)scene;
@end
```

New terms and **important words** are shown in bold. Words that you see on the screen, for example, in menus or dialog boxes, appear in the text like this: "In SpriteBuilder, go to **File | Publish**. This will show a progress bar, and if your project is brand new, it'll go quite fast."

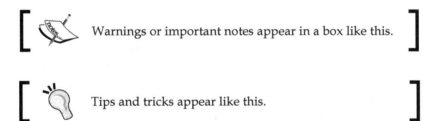

> Warnings or important notes appear in a box like this.

> Tips and tricks appear like this.

Reader feedback

Feedback from our readers is always welcome. Let us know what you think about this book—what you liked or disliked. Reader feedback is important for us as it helps us develop titles that you will really get the most out of.

To send us general feedback, simply e-mail feedback@packtpub.com, and mention the book's title in the subject of your message.

If there is a topic that you have expertise in and you are interested in either writing or contributing to a book, see our author guide at www.packtpub.com/authors.

Customer support

Now that you are the proud owner of a Packt book, we have a number of things to help you to get the most from your purchase.

Downloading the example code

You can download the example code files from your account at http://www.packtpub.com for all the Packt Publishing books you have purchased. If you purchased this book elsewhere, you can visit http://www.packtpub.com/support and register to have the files e-mailed directly to you.

Downloading the color images of this book

We also provide you with a PDF file that has color images of the screenshots/diagrams used in this book. The color images will help you better understand the changes in the output. You can download this file from http://www.packtpub.com/sites/default/files/downloads/6718OS_ColorImages.pdf.

Errata

Although we have taken every care to ensure the accuracy of our content, mistakes do happen. If you find a mistake in one of our books—maybe a mistake in the text or the code—we would be grateful if you could report this to us. By doing so, you can save other readers from frustration and help us improve subsequent versions of this book. If you find any errata, please report them by visiting http://www.packtpub.com/submit-errata, selecting your book, clicking on the **Errata Submission Form** link, and entering the details of your errata. Once your errata are verified, your submission will be accepted and the errata will be uploaded to our website or added to any list of existing errata under the Errata section of that title.

To view the previously submitted errata, go to https://www.packtpub.com/books/content/support and enter the name of the book in the search field. The required information will appear under the **Errata** section.

Piracy

Piracy of copyrighted material on the Internet is an ongoing problem across all media. At Packt, we take the protection of our copyright and licenses very seriously. If you come across any illegal copies of our works in any form on the Internet, please provide us with the location address or website name immediately so that we can pursue a remedy.

Please contact us at copyright@packtpub.com with a link to the suspected pirated material.

We appreciate your help in protecting our authors and our ability to bring you valuable content.

Questions

If you have a problem with any aspect of this book, you can contact us at questions@packtpub.com, and we will do our best to address the problem.

1
Refreshing Your Cocos2d Knowledge

In this chapter, we'll be bringing you up to speed by refreshing the memory of the most advanced users. This chapter will also cover project planning before any project even gets created. You'll see later why determining what features you want early can help speed up the process of creating a game. Project examples, references to downloading, and setup information will be found here. We'll then take a deep dive into the various additional third-party libraries and tools in the Cocos2d ecosystem that you may want to consider.

In this chapter, we will cover the following topics:

- Planning for a successful game
- Additional tools you might want to consider
- Setting flexible, focused goals

Preparing the mindset

First, we'll discuss how to structure your project from start to finish, and why you should do that instead of just jumping right in. We're going to discuss some theory and ask you questions to help you determine what exactly your project will need before even a line of code is written.

Before you start planning, you need to ask questions about key features your game needs, as they will require additional support and development. For example, is there a physics engine involved? Are you going to implement Game Center or In-App Purchases or possibly connect to a database to store the user's information? How complex are the mechanics? Start thinking of the answers to these and similar questions, as knowing the answers will help you move faster and still remain efficient.

The physics engine

Although this is not something that most people will know off the top of their head when they first start planning their project, it's important to know. Luckily, with Cocos2d, there's a physics engine built into the code for you, which is nice because you don't have to go out of your way to implement one.

If you find your project does need a physics engine (or would be much more 'realistic' with it), you can refer to *Chapter 5, Creating Cool Content*, later on in this book to understand how to implement it, as well as example code to use.

If you're unsure of whether you should use a physics engine or not, here are a few examples of games that use Box2D, one of the built-in physics engines with Cocos2d. Take a look at the physics in *Angry Birds* by Rovio:

In the preceding screenshot, each bird and each pig is a circle-shaped physics object, the ground is a rectangle, and all the obstacles on the right-hand side (except the pigs) are rectangles. When the bird gets flung from the left side to the right side, gravity starts acting on the bird and begins pulling it down. Once collisions occur, it pushes the objects around and does some fancy "damage" calculations based on the velocity of the incoming and colliding object.

The following screenshot is of the physics in *Crescent Ridge Mini Golf* by KeitGames:

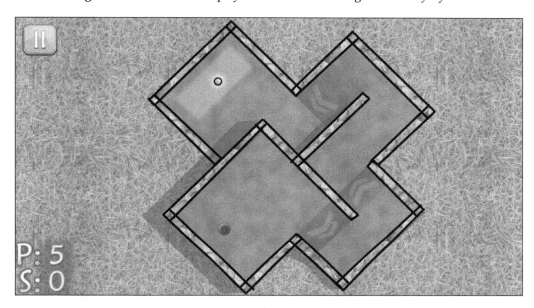

In the preceding screenshot, the ball is a circle-shaped physics object, and each wall has a set of vertices that act as the boundaries through which the ball cannot pass. There is no gravity in play here, or else the ball would be constantly falling to the bottom of the screen. If the ball bounces on a wall, the physics engine knows exactly what angle the ball will turn by, and by what velocity it will go backwards. Being able to determine the angle of reflection of the golf ball was the main reason a physics engine was used to create a simple mini golf game.

If you're still unsure, then answering "yes" to any of the following questions means you should consider using a physics engine. If your answer to any of the following questions is "yes," then refer to *Chapter 3, Focusing on Physics*, to learn how to implement a physics engine. If your answer to all of these questions is "no," then I suggest holding off for now because your game probably doesn't need an engine, and instead, it can be coded in a way that gives the impression of physics but doesn't actually use a physics engine:

- Do you need noncircular or nonrectangular objects to collide?
- Do objects need to bounce off of each other or push other objects?
- Does your game make use of real-time gravity?

If you're interested in making use of any liquid physics or using soft bodies in your game, feel free to check out LiquidFun. However, this book will not cover how to implement or use that engine.

In-App Purchases

In-App Purchases (IAPs) are a feature that are a result of design decisions, possibly to make the game cheaper and/or include expansions or extra content in the game. There are a lot of ways you can utilize IAPs, but forcing them into your game instead of designing them as an integral part of the experience could cause your players to either not utilize the IAPs you took so much time to implement, or just stop playing the game altogether.

The thing about IAPs is that Apple requires your project's provisioning profile to have the IAPs permission added — that's the easy part. The hard part is getting them included in your code. Here are some examples of In-App Purchases in various games. The following screenshot is of the shop in *Clash of Clans* by Supercell:

In the preceding screenshot, you see the various IAPs available in *Clash of Clans*. You can see that they have a tiered structure such that as the player spends more money in one go, they get more gems per dollar spent. The following screenshot is of the bank in *Bina Blocks* by KeitGames:

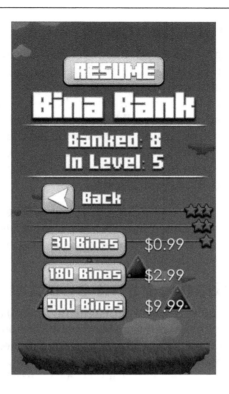

What you just saw is a screenshot of the bank in *Bina Blocks*. You can see a similar tier of pricing as was in *Clash of Clans*.

Although IAP implementation is not covered in this book, it can still be a significant constituent of your game. If you wish to continue learning how to implement your own IAPs, you can read about them from any of these sources:

- `http://www.raywenderlich.com/21081/introduction-to-in-app-purchases-in-ios-6-tutorial`

- `http://www.playngive.com/blog/2010/3/6/adding-in-app-store-to-cocos2d.html`

- `http://troybrant.net/blog/2010/01/in-app-purchases-a-full-walkthrough/`

Making use of analytics

Analytics packages are a great tool that any developer can make use of. If you want to know what level your users are getting stuck at the most, you can track how many times each level was beaten to see where the drop-off happens. Or maybe, you want to track how people are using the new characters you just added. In *Chapter 7, Reaching Our Destination*, you'll learn how to implement Flurry Analytics, which uses a simple, event-driven system used to track when certain methods get called. Essentially, you can track anything from a button press and screen loading to the time a user spent on a problem. All of this data is sent to Flurry's server and compiled into easy-to-read charts and graphs.

Although your users won't notice any difference, it'll definitely make your game better in the long run, as you can see what is happening when your players interact with your game. Thus, you can submit better updates as time goes on.

Complex mechanics and special effects

The term "complex mechanics" can be a bit vague or general at times. However, it can be anything from a really smooth transition between your game's scenes to a unique control system for the way the player plays the game. If you feel that your game needs these complex mechanics to become successful, them make sure you do it right. If you're only planning to add extra bells and whistles because you feel that you have to, and not because it's part of making your game better, then thinking of this beforehand can help structure your project plan in a way that allows the addition of extra (or bonus) features at the end of development. This is better than attempting to add things halfway through and delaying necessary features if you can't figure out how to code them right away.

There are some games that are very special because of their unique gameplay mechanics, in combination with making use of the touch screen (which we will cover in detail in *Chapter 4, Sounding Off*). For example, if you look at *Smash Hit*, *Blek*, *Tiny Wings*, or *Threes!*, you'll see that they don't quite fit into any traditional genre.

Note that if you're relatively new to game design (especially when it comes to mobile design), it might not be entirely in your best interest to try something completely new or unique. Instead, try at least replicating mechanics that already exist, and possibly tweaking them slightly to better fit the game that you're trying to make. The following screenshot is of *Smash Hit*:

The next screenshot is of *Blek*:

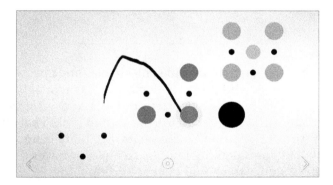

The following screenshot is of *Tiny Wings*:

This screenshot is of *Threes!*:

These are games that thrive on their complex mechanics and special effects. They were extremely well-planned and properly designed. If you're only looking for special effects (for example, particle explosions or faces on the *Threes!* cards), then *Chapter 7, Reaching Our Destination*, is where you should look. That chapter goes into detail of how to polish your game and increase its likeability factor. But for now, just know that if you plan to do something unique, creative, or never done before as an integral part of your design, you should plan accordingly.

If you are adding mechanics just because you think it would be cool to have it and it isn't necessary for the game's progression, then plan it at the end. There's nothing worse than delaying your game's launch date because of a feature that isn't really that important in the first place.

Choosing tools and getting started

Knowing which tools your project is going to need before you start working is a good place to start. In this way, when the time comes to implement a given feature, you can easily open the program and use the tool you've gotten beforehand. It's not too bad to get the tools halfway through the project, but from experience, it's better to think of it before you start to work on a project.

There are a few third-party programs out there that make development of games using Cocos2d go a lot faster. Listed here are such products, information on how to download and install them, along with their cost (if any) and other things you need to know about them.

 Note that just because a product is listed here does not mean it is required when creating a game using Cocos2d. This section is merely a "just in case you were wondering" guide for things to consider when trying to develop better, more polished games.

This section also assumes that you either have a dedicated person creating the artwork for your game, or you will be doing it yourself in any image editing software, such as Photoshop. This is assumed because there are no listed image editors here due to the large volume of editors. Any of them can be used when making games. However, the programs listed here are the best at what they strive to do, although there may be others similar to them.

- **Texture Packer**: This is an image condenser used to place all your images on one sprite sheet. This helps draw optimization (increases your game's frames per second) as well as reduces the space in your game's overall size (which could mean the difference between the users having to download over Wi-Fi, or not).

- **Particle Designer**: This is a visual particle editor that allows quick creation of particle effects, ranging from lasers and smoke effects to explosions and candle effects.

- **Glyph Designer**: This is a custom font creator that allows you to create nice-looking fonts instead of using pre-rendered images with text or plain fonts with just a fill color.

- **VertexHelper Pro**: This is a visual vertex calculator meant for use with physics engines. It can be used for other purposes, but it's mostly used in conjunction with a physics engine to determine the exact coordinates of collision, instead of using a standard box or circle to calculate the collision boundaries of an object.

- **GAF**: This is a way to store Flash animation in an open cross-platform format for further playback in a multitude of game development frameworks and devices. GAF enables artists and animators to use Flash CS to create complex animations and seamlessly use them with various game development frameworks such as Cocos2d, Cocos2d-x, Unity3D, and Starling, to name a few.

- **Git and GitHub/Bitbucket**: There are many ways to make use of source control when working on a project. The best solution out there, as well as the one that many developers use, is Git. You can manage your code changes over time, and if a bug ever shows up, you can always revert to your latest version of your code without losing precious development time trying to figure out what was changed. It's also a nice way to back up your project in case of computer failure.

TexturePacker

TexturePacker allows you to easily create sprite sheets for your games. It compresses your individual images into one giant image so that you can effectively increase the optimization of your game without sacrificing quality.

The final sheets can be used in a variety of game engines such as Cocos2d, Unity, Corona SDK, SpriteKit, and many more. The following screenshot shows the UI of TexturePacker:

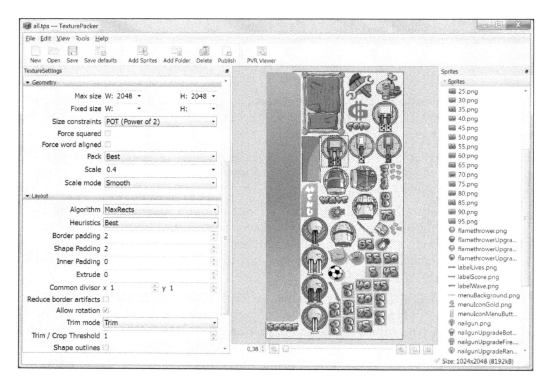

The cost is \$39.95 for the Pro version (free trial available).

To download TexturePacker, go to `http://www.codeandweb.com/texturepacker/download`. There, you can click on the name of the OS you are using, and you're on your way!

TexturePacker is offered on Mac 10.7/8/9, Linux (Ubuntu 64-bit), and Windows 32-bit and 64-bit (XP/Vista/7/8).

Particle Designer

If you want that beautiful explosion, that awesome smoke effect, or that shiny laser beam generated in real time, then Particle Designer is what you need. Import your own custom "particle," change a ton of parameters to get the effect you want, and export the file to your game project. The following screenshot shows the UI of Particle Designer:

The cost is \$74.99 (free trial available)

To download Particle Designer, go to `https://71squared.com/particledesigner`. There, you will see a link to buy it. You can, however, get a trial version by clicking on the **Try** button on their website and entering your e-mail address.

Particle Designer is offered on Mac 10.8, 9, and 10.

Technically, you can manually create each particle in the code, but that's horribly inefficient. Plus, being able to see the particle in real time as you're designing it makes the entire process smoother, as importing the particle effect to Cocos2d is extremely easy.

If you have Particle Designer but haven't used it before, you're advised to just open it up and start messing around with some of the settings. You can get some seriously cool effects just by dragging some sliders around.

Glyph Designer

If you want fancy fonts instead of the normal TrueType fonts available, or a pre-rendered image of text in Photoshop for example, you can use Glyph Designer. It basically allows you to get a nicely styled character set that can be used with the BMFont labels (bitmap fonts). This essentially means that you can generate custom text labels while still maintaining the colorful, styled font you've created using Glyph Designer.

Its cost is $39.99 (free trial available).

To download Glyph Designer go to `https://71squared.com/en/glyphdesigner`. There, you will see a link to buy it. You can, however, get a trial version by clicking on the **Try** button on their website and entering your e-mail address.

Glyph Designer is offered on Mac 10.8, 9, and 10.

If you want fonts like those used in some of the games whose screenshots you saw earlier (*Clash of Clans*, *Angry Birds*, *Crescent Ridge Mini Golf*, and *Bina Blocks*), instead of just plain, solid-colored fonts as shown in the other games, you'll need a good bitmap font creation tool. Just as with particles, if you want to get nice-looking fonts, there are only a few programs out there. One of them is Glyph Designer, which was made by the same people who created Particle Designer.

If you have Glyph Designer installed but haven't begun using it yet, open it and begin testing some different styles on various fonts just to get a feel for how the program works and some of the things you can create with Glyph Designer.

One thing to consider when designing your aesthetics (and especially when it comes to choosing custom fonts) is, does this font/style work within the overall aesthetics of the entire project? If it feels jarring or feels like two different styles clashing, then it might be in your best interest to choose a more suitable font for your game. Don't worry; it might not come to you right away, but if you find the right font, it adds that extra layer of polishing that's crucial to making your game a success (we'll talk more about polishing in *Chapter 6, Tidying Up and Polishing*).

VertexHelper

Are you using physics in the game? Do you need a shape better than a box or a circle to represent a complex object? VertexHelper can help you find the coordinates that make up the shape of a complex object by importing an image and allowing you to click where you want the vertices to be. You can manually guess and test the coordinates programmatically if you really want, but VertexHelper makes this process a lot faster and keeps the coordinates accurate (assuming that the physics is implemented properly in the code).

If you're going to make use of physics (or collisions in general), you should be aware that vertex collisions can be incredibly expensive. If possible, it's best to stick to primitives (for example, circles or squares), And if that's the case, it may be that you don't even need a physics engine. Hence, consider your options carefully.

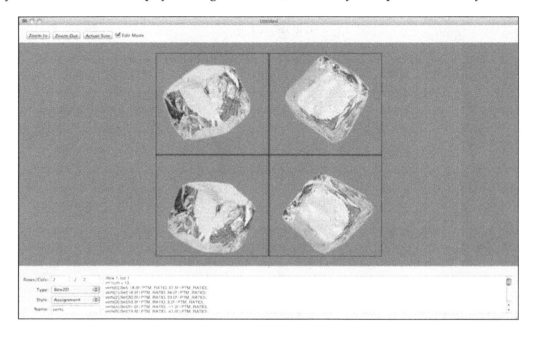

Its cost is $7.99.

To download go to https://itunes.apple.com/us/app/vertexhelper-pro/id411684411, or search for VertexHelper Pro and you should be able to find the link to the Mac App Store on the first page of results.

Like any other Mac app, you can run this once it is fully installed.

There are two ways to go about generating your boundaries for any physics object:

- Manually code the values using b2Vec2 arrays and hope that it's correct
- Use a program such as VertexHelper to quickly create boundaries for each object

It's good to know about this program and have it ready when using a physics engine in your game because every object pretty much needs to collide with another object (except a few background images, most likely). With that said, every object probably isn't a square or a circle so being able to create custom-shaped physics boundaries very quickly is good.

If you do have VertexHelper installed on your computer, go ahead; open it and import an image. Then start clicking around and get a feel for how the program works. This will help a lot later on as you start to implement the physics of each object.

GAF

If you have any Flash animation that you want to convert for use in your games made with Cocos2d, you can do so with GAF, which is essentially a single format that gets converted into the individual framework's and device's requirements.

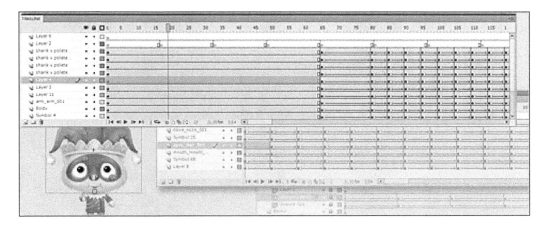

Its cost is as follows: for the Free version, $0; for Studio, $995; and for Enterprise, $2,995. Free use is limited to $50,000 annually, and you can develop only your own games, not contract work. You can read more about their pricing options at `http://gafmedia.com/pricing`.

To download GAF go to `http://gafmedia.com/downloads` and choose the OS. Then follow the instructions to install.

GAF is available on both Windows and OSX.

GAF can be helpful if you have an art developer who is comfortable with animating in SWF files, and can then convert them into a platform-agnostic format for use with multiple game engines. It can also be helpful if you're porting a game that already makes use of SWF files (such as an online Flash game that you wish to implement on mobiles).

Git and GitHub/Bitbucket

If you're ever working with code, chances are that something's going to get messed up. Luckily, there is source control software that exists to manage your code's versioning and ensuring that in case anything goes wrong, you have copies of previous versions to revert to.

This is a screenshot of the Cocos2d-Swift GitHub repository (or repo for short) at `https://github.com/cocos2d/cocos2d-swift`:

It is free of cost.

To download this, if you have Xcode installed on your Mac, simply go to **Xcode | Preferences | Downloads**. Then install the command-line tools. With this, you can use Xcode's built-in **Source Control** menu, or go through Terminal to use your Git commands.

If you wish to install Git manually, simply go to their website and follow the links to download and install, at `http://git-scm.com/`.

Note that if you've never used any source control before, feel free to read how it works at `https://help.github.com/`.

You will actually need Git installed only on your Mac, as that's where the code is. However, you can install it on any desktop OS.

Both GitHub and Bitbucket are free to use. However, the key difference is that GitHub offers unlimited public repositories, while Bitbucket offers unlimited private repositories. So if you want to keep your code hidden from others while still making use of the services listed, it's recommended to go with Bitbucket.

Both of these services use Git and make use of the same commands and tools. It's just a preference between whether you want to go with public or private repositories (or the case where someone else you work with has a preference).

Setting flexible, focused goals

When you first came up with your idea to make a game, you probably thought it was the best game idea since the beginning of gaming. It honestly might be; don't let my words hold you back. However, as time passes, your vision of this game might change and your direction might shift a little or a lot as new ideas are generated throughout the project's life cycle. It's best to come up with a focused goal that's also a bit flexible to leave room for improvement while staying on track when it gets too much out of hand.

Expand

If you're struggling with coming up with an original idea, I recommend that you get a whiteboard (the bigger the better; trust me), open an image editing software on your computer, or even get some pens and paper, and just start writing down whatever you want to make a game about. Pick a topic related to the game's genre, or synonyms related to the main mechanics involved, and start making a map (something like a spider web) of ideas that you can use in the initial phase of creating your game.

However, creating the initial idea can be tough on its own; for example, when is a project ever really ready such that you can begin the coding or the art creation process? Is it after the first mechanics implementation? Or is it when each of the 27 levels is methodically mapped from start to finish? It's important to realize that moment when you've stopped expanding and improving the game, which is getting better as you come up with more ideas, and you're coming up with ideas just because you can.

Focus

Once you have a good idea of the type of game you want to make, it's time to focus that end goal in such a way that it allows flexibility later. In my honest opinion, making games is all about flow and the creation of ideas as time passes by. So, if you're in the middle of making a game and you think adding another enemy type or a few side quests might make the game more interesting, then don't hesitate to do so.

That said, you can't be flip-flopping all over the place from one idea to the next, or else your game will lack a sense of direction as the player goes through it. They will feel as if the plot never resolves the initial conflicts presented.

Plus, if your game lacks a focused end goal and is constantly changing over time, it will just take longer to develop. So, speaking from experience, if you want to create two different game ideas, the second of which is something you thought would be cool halfway through the development of the first game, either add it in as an update or expansion after the first game is released, or turn it into a separate project, but don't delay the development longer than it already has to.

So what are some of the things you should have in a focused goal? If your game has a narrative or is somehow plot driven, try to ensure that this stays intact throughout the development. Or, if your game is dependent on a single feature of mechanics and you want to add another feature halfway through the game, ensure that the newly added feature does not affect the initial user experience that was thought about when first coming up with the idea of the game. However, if the feature you want to add isn't really that important for the initial part of the game, then don't worry about it now and just include it in an update. Trust me; unless it's going take a few minutes to add the new feature, it's probably not worth spending your time on something that's not very necessary for the game to work as intended when it was first designed. Or, if the art style of the game just isn't very appealing or could be represented in another way, think about how important the art really is for your game. If it's low-quality art, as done in MS Paint for example, then consider getting some higher-quality art. However, if it's already polished, then don't bother changing it until after the release.

Flex

I've mentioned in the preceding section: do not hesitate to be a bit lenient when it comes to your game's mechanics, narrative, art style, and so on. As your game progresses, you will almost inevitably think, "Oh my gosh, wouldn't it be the best game in the world if we just added this one extra boss at the end?" Maybe, it will. And that's where you would want to be flexible.

But remember to try staying true to that focused goal we talked about in the previous section. It's all about keeping that balance between laser-focused goals and free-flowing creativity at every step of the way.

Downloading the IDE and Source Code

If you don't have Xcode and the Cocos2d library installed on your computer, now is probably a good time to do that. This section will guide you through the process.

Step 1 – become a developer through Apple's iOS program

Now, it's not entirely necessary for this book to pay the $99 per year fee to become an official Apple iOS developer. But if you wish to test the apps and games on your device or release the apps to the App Store, it is required.

If you wish to skip this step for now, feel free. You can get back here when you're ready.

First, go to `https://developer.apple.com/programs/start/standard/` to begin your enrollment process for the iOS App Developer program. If you already have an Apple account, you may use it if you wish. Otherwise, create an account.

Next, choose either **Individual** or **Company**. Apple provides a nice description on their website, so I feel that if you need help determining which one to get, their site can aid you in making that decision.

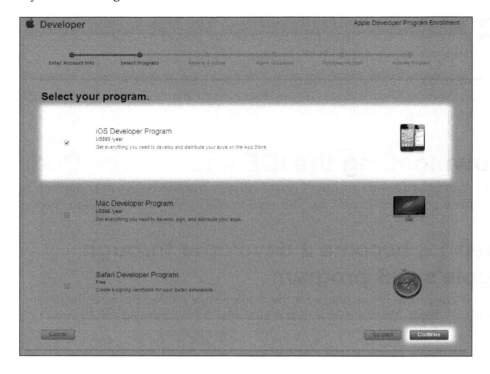

Go through the steps to enter some contact information, then select **iOS Developer Program**, and click on **Continue**.

Agree to the license, enter your purchasing information, and you're on your way!

Step 2 – download and install Xcode

Go to `https://developer.apple.com/xcode/downloads/` and click on the link to download Xcode. At the time of writing this book, it says **View in the Mac App Store**, and the version of Xcode referenced in this book is Xcode 6. It requires OS X 10.9.3.

Like a regular app from the Mac App Store, it should be installed in your `Applications` folder, and you should be able to be run it after the installation.

Adding a device

Note that if you want to run your app on a device, it requires a developer account (which was talked about in the *Step 1 – become a developer through Apple's iOS program* section). If you already have it set up, you should be able to add your device to your developer account by going to **Window | Organizer** in Xcode, and clicking on **Devices**.

Under that, you should see your device's name, and a button in the main view that says **Use for Development**.

If it is not showing, but instead giving a message like **The version of iOS on "Brian's iPhone" is not supported by this installation ...**, it means you must install the latest version of Xcode to get the latest version of the SDK so that your device can be properly supported.

Step 3 – download Cocos2d (via SpriteBuilder)

Go to http://www.cocos2d-swift.org/download and click on the download link under Latest Release, labelled SpriteBuilder (this should open the Mac App Store). At the time of writing this book, the latest version is **Cocos2D 3.2.1**, so any content in this book will be following that version unless stated otherwise (for example, version 2.1).

As of version 3.2, Cocos2d can be installed only by using SpriteBuilder. For those unfamiliar with SpriteBuilder, let me tell you that it is used to create projects with a drag-and-drop interface. You do not need to create your game entirely through SpriteBuilder. However, as of Cocos2D 3.2.1, project creation is possible only through SpriteBuilder.

As with any Mac app, this will be downloaded on your \Applications folder, and can be run once fully installed.

Creating a new project via SpriteBuilder

Once Xcode and SpriteBuilder are installed, we can set up an initial project to see it all in action. Cocos2d is nice enough to give us some initial temporary files on a project creation so that we can get a better start. It's nice because we can basically replace them with our own files once we need to.

Open **SpriteBuilder**. It may ask you to join their mailing list, but it doesn't make a difference in this book whether you sign up or not.

After that, it may look as if a new project has already been started (which may be the case, but let's make sure we start fresh). Go to **File | New | Project**, and choose a folder location you will remember (for example, \Desktop or \Documents). It should then open up a preview with a blue backdrop and the SpriteBuilder text, as shown in the following screenshot:

Do not be alarmed if you do not see this exact message. It is simply what's happening in version 1.2.1 of SpriteBuilder at the time of writing this book.

Congratulations! Your project is now set up.

If you wish to start creating your project using the SpriteBuilder visual editor for Cocos2d, you can now do so. However, this book does not include any tutorials on how to use the program, so if you wish to learn how this program works and all about the full potential of the visual editor, check out https://www. makegameswith.us/tutorials/getting-started-with-spritebuilder/. They have a great set of tutorials on SpriteBuilder.

If you wish to start coding instead of dragging and dropping, follow the steps in the next section.

Exporting SpriteBuilder projects to Xcode

In SpriteBuilder, go to **File | Publish**. This will show a progress bar, and if your project is brand new, it'll go quite fast.

By default, the Xcode files that are generated when the **Publish** button is pressed get saved in the same folder as the project location you chose when you first created the project. Remember that I told you to save it in a place that you'll remember? Go back to that location, either in **Finder** or by going to **Xcode | Open viewer**.

Find the file with the same name as your project. It should look something like this:

```
ProjectName.xcodeproj
```

If you do not see the .xcodepoj file extension, don't worry. It should be labelled as Xcode project in the kind filter and have a blueprint icon next to it.

Click on that to open it. It should bring up Xcode.

Feel free to either run the app in a simulator of your choice or attach a device and give it a go. Looking good so far! If you wish to run the app on a device, go to the section in this chapter titled *Adding a device*.

Summary

We looked at how to plan your game according to the specific elements you wish to include in it, how to choose the tools you'll be needing along the way as you create your game, as well as some best practices when it comes to actually creating the idea and moving forward throughout the project's lifetime.

Finally, we covered how to download and install Xcode, downloaded and installed SpriteBuilder, and downloaded various third-party applications that make your life much easier.

The next chapter will cover in depth why prototypes are essential for a great game design, why failing faster with quickly iterated prototypes is the key, and why creating a minimal viable product that people can actually play (even if it's buggier than anything you've ever seen) is very important for your game's long-term success.

2
Failing Faster with Prototypes

This chapter is all about getting a wireframe of the project going so that you can fill in the "meat" of the game later. You'll be getting baseline graphics, menus, and the game's flow structure outlined for testing faster than you can blink. Test sooner, fail faster — this is your new motto as a game developer. Even though it may seem very simple to code, that's our intent: to create the minimum viable product — something tangible and working — as soon as possible in order to get a feel of the overall project. We're going to cover the following in this chapter:

- Why prototype?
- Getting a scene up and running
- Creating text (labels)
- Beginning using sprite sheets with TexturePacker
- Creating buttons
- Creating menus, scenes, and scene transitions
- Creating nodes and units (sprites)

Throughout this book, a complete game will be created from beginning to end, starting with this chapter. Creating an ongoing project will serve two purposes, as follows:

- Show how each section can fit within a full project and not just as a piece of code all on its own
- Visualize the process of an entire project from the beginning to the end without skipping any step

In the files included with this book, you can find the finished project to see what it's going to look and feel like. Also, at the beginning of each chapter, there will be a reference to the version of the project up to that point in the book so that you can follow along with the complete explanation/examples in the book.

> At this point, the project is created as a fresh project by following the tutorial in *Chapter 1, Refreshing Our Cocos2d Knowledge*. If you would rather use a default starting point, you can use the project in the blank `Project` folder in the files included with this book.
>
> You can also download the code from `https://github.com/keitzer/MasteringCocos2d`.

File suffixes versus directories

When Cocos2d and SpriteBuilder became integrated in Cocos2d 3.0, they changed the way textures are read in by Cocos2d. In previous versions, if you wanted to make a game for the iPhone and the iPad, you had to add various suffixes to your file. For example, if your image was named `btnPlay.png`, you had to create variously sized files in your project, which were named as follows:

- `btnPlay.png`
- `btnPlay-hd.png`
- `btnPlay-ipad.png`
- `btnPlay-ipadhd.png`

This methodology of getting your files saved is typically referred to as using **file suffixes**.

In the newer iteration of Cocos2d with SpriteBuilder, one of the ways you can manage your textures is by dragging a file of the largest possible size (for example, Retina iPad) into SpriteBuilder. When you click on **Publish**, SpriteBuilder will take care of the file size variations for you. This way of handling files is referred to as using **directories**.

> Here is a warning: if you decide to manually add files to the `Published-iOS` folder, do not click on **Clean Cache** in SpriteBuilder, or else you will lose all of those files.

However, using directories has its drawbacks. For example, you may want to use TexturePacker (which we will use later in this chapter, as well as throughout the book), but there is no easy way to use it and the new directory style of saving files. You technically can, but it's such a pain that any advantage TexturePacker has is negated by the extra work you have to do. So TexturePacker can work with the directory style of file reading. Thus, it's just easier to drag the files into SpriteBuilder if you're going to use the directory style.

So how will we work around this problem if we want to take advantage of TexturePacker? Well, until there exists a version of Cocos2d and SpriteBuilder that integrates the use of TexturePacker, we have to go back to the file suffix method.

 Note that if you do not wish to purchase TexturePacker, don't worry; it's not required. The later code will stay the same, as Cocos2d searches for the image, whether it was loaded via sprite sheets or as an individual file. If you do not wish to use TexturePacker, feel free to avoid changing your search mode (as mentioned next) and just go ahead with the directory method. Whenever this book mentions adding a file to the sprite sheet, that's your queue to add it to SpriteBuilder.

Since Cocos2d 3.0 and higher versions use the directory method by default, and since we're going to switch to using file extensions, we must look up the Xcode project for **CCFileUtilsSearchModeDirectory**. One of the results should be a file called CCBReader.m. Click on the result and it should take you to approximately line 109, where you'll see the following line of code:

```
sharedFileUtils.searchMode = CCFileUtilsSearchModeDirectory;
```

You're going to change that line to use the suffix search mode:

```
sharedFileUtils.searchMode = CCFileUtilsSearchModeSuffix;//
CCFileUtilsSearchModeDirectory;
```

With that in place, we're ready to begin the prototype phase of our project. But first, why is it important to make a prototype? And why is it important to create it quickly? Why not just code the game slowly and eventually get the core mechanics of the game in whenever it's time?

Why prototype?

Besides the obvious reason of asking your friends "is it fun?!" before it's fully complete, prototyping your game, especially quickly and early on in development, can be very useful for a few different reasons:

- You can ask about the originality/innovation of your game from the perspective of an end user instead of just your own views

- You can generate ideas on how to improve the game way before it's too late to make changes

- You can get a feel of how the game actually flows from one stage to the next, and conceive a tangible product instead of just an idea

- If shown to the public, it could be a great way to begin the marketing of your game and beginning the snowball of exposure needed to succeed on iOS

Plus, this is the best way to start a project, especially a project that includes new concepts or ideas that might be hard to get fully coded and work as intended. You might have heard of the term **proof of concept**; this chapter is exactly what that is. It's a very quick overview of your entire game that you can show to others and ask, "This is proof that I can make this concept into a full-blown game. What do you think?"

Now that you've understood why making a prototype for your game is a good idea, let's quickly go over the project this book will be covering.

Playtesting and feedback analysis

When you have your prototype ready for others to experience, it's best to go out and actually get some people to play your game. Ideally, you should find playtesters who are knowledgeable in that game's genre as well as within the age range of your game's target audience so that they can give quality feedback.

The feedback you receive will vary from "Wow! This is amazing!" to "I don't understand how to play this game." You have to be prepared to hear all kinds of responses. Also, just because someone says your game is bad might not necessarily mean it is bad. However, if what they're saying is objectively true, and implementing what they have to say will improve your players' experience, then you should listen to their opinion as it will make not only your current game but also future games better.

Anyway, let's get into actually making a project that others can play.

Project for the book

To get an idea of the project this book will be going through, imagine a 9 x 9 grid with your "base" at the center and enemies spawning around the squares at the edges. It's a turn-based game. On each turn, every unit moves one square. Each unit has a number that increases by one every turn. If your unit collides with the enemy's unit, the two numbers subtract and whichever unit has a positive result stays alive. Your goal is to protect your main base from an enemy unit, surviving an attack on your main base for as many turns as you can.

Here are a few screenshots of the finished game (by the end of *Chapter 7, Reaching Our Destination*):

When the game first starts up, it will look like what is shown in the following screenshot:

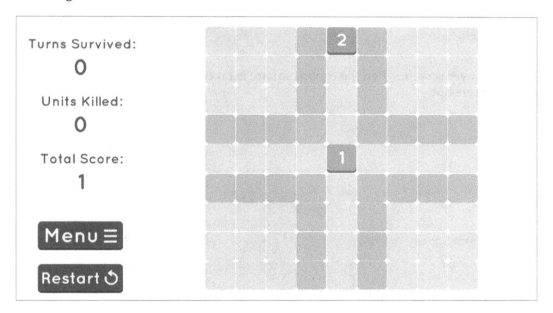

The game midway through a session will look as follows:

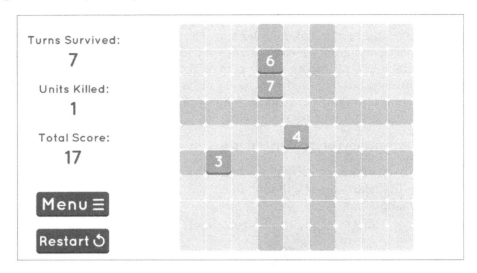

The game over screen, when the central square is taken, will look like what is shown in this screenshot:

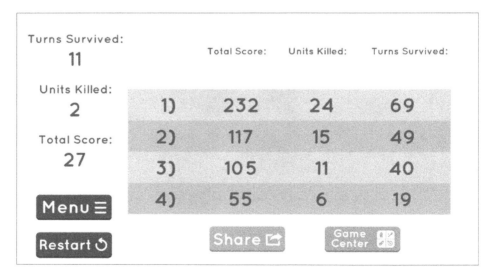

A quick mock-up

Whether it's Photoshop, Illustrator, MS Paint, a paper and a pencil, a whiteboard, crayons, or any other creative way to draw your ideas, it's best to get a visual of the project so that when you begin to code, you at least have a basis for why you're choosing the colors and text positions that you are choosing.

Moreover, even though we have screenshots of the finished product, which we just saw, we need to imagine where to start. For example, in the following screenshot, you'll see a quick mock-up made for this book's project, as described earlier. The dimensions are 2048 x 1536 (iPad landscape). It was done relatively quickly for the purpose of showing the game as a concept, not as a finished product that is meant for marketing purposes. Don't worry; yours doesn't have to look as good as this if your art skills are lacking.

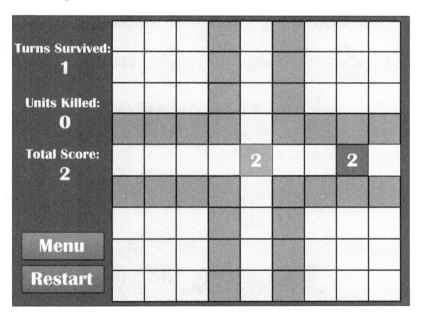

This is an example of a great starting point because it doesn't have any menus or fancy transitions; just the game. I know there's a button that says **Menu**, but that's intended for later use, when we actually implement the menu. Remember, a prototype is supposed to be quick. It doesn't matter if the graphics, colors, fonts, or even the menu placements or word choices change. The point is to get it up as fast as possible. *Test sooner, fail faster.*

Overview of how the Cocos2d engine works

Before we go too deep into the code, let's quickly go over how the Cocos2d engine works. If you're using Cocos2d for the first time, this should be helpful. If you've used Cocos2d before, feel free to read through this, as it might be a refresher for you.

Cocos2d is essentially a series of parents and children. The base parent is the currently running scene. You can have only one scene displayed at any given time. Within the scene, there will be children, all of which have to be of the CCNode type. A CCNode object is an object that has a position, rotation, scale, color, and various other properties. A CCNode object can have other CCNode objects added to it.

Each subclass of CCNode inherits from it and adds functionality on top of the CCNode class. For example, if we want to draw an image on the screen, we'll use CCSprite, which is essentially a CCNode object, but with an image attached. Even a scene (type of CCScene) is a subclass of CCNode (which is how each scene can have children).

Here's an image made to help describe the relationship between parents and children within Cocos2d. First, we have the individual images we want to display on the screen, in a very simple texture atlas.

Next, we have a diagram of an example of CCScene. Added to the scene are five CCSprite objects: the sky, the two trees, the road, and the player.

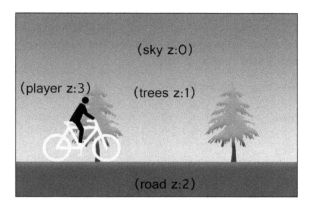

The sky is positioned at z-index equal to 0, the trees at z-index equal to 1 (which means they'll be displayed in front of the sky), the road at z-index equal to 2 (which means it'll be displayed in front of both the sky and the trees), and the player at z-index equal to 3 (which means it'll be displayed in front of everything). The default z-index is 0.

Everything else in Cocos2d is simple—just a CCNode object with other CCNode objects added as children.

Here's one thing to remember about the parent-child relationship that Cocos2d uses: if you move a parent by 20 points, for example, the children will also be moved by the same amount.

Now that we've briefly gone over how Cocos2d works, let's get our prototype going.

Getting a scene up and running

Before we even start adding anything to the screen, we need to make sure we have a game that can be viewed on our device or a simulator. Once you've created the project in SpriteBuilder (or gotten the blank project that was listed earlier) and opened the project in Xcode, go to the next step.

Creating the initial code for the scene to open

You should see a file called `MainScene.h` and another file called `MainScene.m`. Open the header file (which has the `.h` extension).

In the header file, add a few lines of code between the `@interface` line and the `@end` line. The header should look like this:

```
@interface MainScene : CCNode
{
   CGSize winSize;
}
+(CCScene*)scene;
@end
```

Then, in the main file (which has the `.m` extension), some lines of code should be added between the `@implementation` and `@end` lines. It should look as follows:

```
#import "MainScene.h"

@implementation MainScene

+(CCScene *)scene
{
   return [[self alloc] init];
}

-(id)init
{
   if ((self=[super init]))
   {
    //used for positioning items on screen
     winSize = [[CCDirector sharedDirector] viewSize];

     float grey = 70 / 255.f;
    //these values range 0 to 1.0, so use float to get ratio
     CCNode *background = [CCNodeColor nodeWithColor:[CCColor
colorWithRed:grey green:grey blue:grey]];
```

```
    [self addChild:background];
  }
  return self;
}

@end
```

Finally, open the `AppDelegate.m` file and scroll to the bottom, where you should see a line in the `startScene` method that looks like this:

```
return [CCBReader loadAsScene:@"MainScene"];
```

We're going to change it to the following:

```
return [MainScene scene];
```

The code might give you an error for this line. This can be fixed by importing the `MainScene` header to the AppDelegate's main file. Simply add this to the top of the `AppDelegate.m` file:

```
#import "MainScene.h"
```

Once all of this has been put in place, feel free to run your project on either your device or the simulator built into Xcode. You can read more about each option in the following sections.

Run it on the simulator – doesn't require an iOS developer license

Running on the simulator is good for testing devices you don't own. For example, if you own an iPhone 5s and want to test how your game looks on an iPhone 6 or 6 Plus, simply load that simulator and test to see how the game looks.

 Note that it's best to test for performance on the device only. Do not test for performance on the simulator. You will never get a perfect representation of the device's capabilities when running on the simulator. Also, you should test only how the game looks.

For testing on the simulator, simply choose which device you wish to simulate from the simulators available in Xcode as shown in the following screenshot:

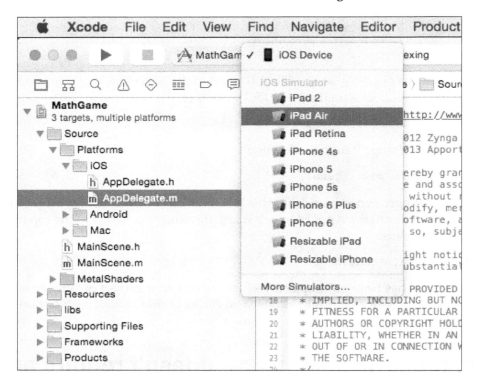

Choose any simulator you want, preferably a simulator that your game will eventually be supported on, and either press the play button on the left, or hit *command + R* to run it. It might take a few minutes to open the simulator, so be patient. But once it does, it should automatically open on the simulator. If it doesn't, just try rerunning it with the simulator already open.

Congratulations! If you have used the simulator, you now have a project that runs! Next, we are going to go over how to run it on device.

Run it on the device – requires an iOS developer license

If you're unsure whether you want to run your game on a device or on the simulator, let me explain why the device is the king in terms of testing purposes. Not only do you get to see and feel the project just as any other user would, but you also get to experience the actual performance of the device rather than a simulated version of it. Plus, if your project is heavy on touchscreen usage (which it honestly should, or else it probably shouldn't be an iOS title), then you can effectively test the feel of the game.

For testing on the device, simply plug in your device. Its name should be listed in Xcode, like this:

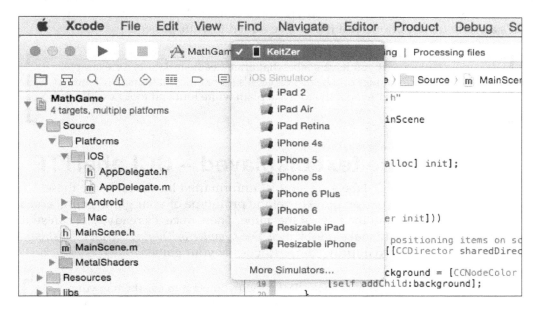

If you do not see the name of your device, make sure you select the iOS device target, and not any of the simulators. If your device is plugged in and it still shows **iOS Device**, make sure you have a developer account subscription in Xcode. Refer to *Chapter 1, Refreshing Our Cocos2d Knowledge*, for more details on this.

Once you see the name of your device, either press the **Play** button on the left, or hit *command + R* to run it. It might take a minute or so to build, but once it's complete, the project will automatically open on your device.

Congratulations! You now have a project that runs. Now we can start adding some content, such as text and buttons, and then move on to creating another scene and transitioning to that and back to the original.

Creating buttons and text (labels)

If you want to place a line of text on the screen, you need to create a label. There are two types of labels in Cocos2d: CCLabelBMFont and CCLabelTTF. Bitmap Font labels are the fancy labels created with Glyph Designer, mentioned earlier in this book. TrueType Font labels are regular, unformatted text labels that use either a font file that's already on the phone or a file you've added to your project.

Note that if you have a label that often needs updating, for example, a score counter or a health value, it's more efficient to use BMFonts in those cases, even if the font is a plain white font and looks exactly the same in TTF format.

Let's get some text displayed – CCLabelTTF

As mentioned earlier, TTF labels are simple, unformatted labels. How are these useful? The answer is, you can quickly get the prototype of your game going, and so you can better understand the flow of the game. Then, once it's ready, you can switch over to using BMFonts to make it look nice. See *Chapter 6, Tidying Up and Polishing*, to learn more about ways to improve the aesthetics of your game.

Here's a short note about BMFonts: if you want to use them in your game, which you should do for performance reasons alone, keep in mind the various limitations that BMFonts have and TTF fonts don't. The first is poor quality when upscaling the label. Then, BMFonts can use only the characters that are in the font atlas, and any foreign language support might mean a lot of extra BMFonts, which could add up quickly in terms of space.

The first thing we're going to do is get those labels on the left side going. The following code should be added to MainScene.h (the lbl prefix in the front of the variable will indicate to us that it's a label; similarly, btn for button, num for number, and so on):

```
@interface MainScene : CCNode
{
  CGSize winSize;
  //Add the following:
  //the labels used for displaying the game info
  CCLabelTTF *lblTurnsSurvived, *lblUnitsKilled, *lblTotalScore;
}
```

The following code goes into the init method of MainScene.m and will create the labels. We then want to set the position for each label because the default position is in the bottom-left corner. Finally, we add each label to the scene. Remember, the scene is just a node that can have as many children as you want:

```
CCLabelTTF *lblTurnsSurvivedDesc = [CCLabelTTF labelWithString:@"Turns
Survived:" fontName:@"Arial" fontSize:12];
lblTurnsSurvivedDesc.position = ccp(winSize.width * 0.1,
winSize.height * 0.8);
[self addChild:lblTurnsSurvivedDesc];

lblTurnsSurvived = [CCLabelTTF labelWithString:@"0"
fontName:@"Arial" fontSize:22];
lblTurnsSurvived.position = ccp(winSize.width * 0.1,
winSize.height * 0.75);
[self addChild:lblTurnsSurvived];

CCLabelTTF *lblUnitsKilledDesc = [CCLabelTTF labelWithString:@"Units
Killed:" fontName:@"Arial" fontSize:12];
lblUnitsKilledDesc.position = ccp(winSize.width * 0.1, winSize.height
* 0.6);
[self addChild:lblUnitsKilledDesc];

lblUnitsKilled = [CCLabelTTF labelWithString:@"0" fontName:@"Arial"
fontSize:22];
lblUnitsKilled.position = ccp(winSize.width * 0.1, winSize.height *
0.55);
[self addChild:lblUnitsKilled];
```

```
CCLabelTTF *lblTotalScoreDesc = [CCLabelTTF labelWithString:@"Total
Score:" fontName:@"Arial" fontSize:12];
lblTotalScoreDesc.position = ccp(winSize.width * 0.1, winSize.height *
0.4);
[self addChild:lblTotalScoreDesc];

lblTotalScore = [CCLabelTTF labelWithString:@"1" fontName:@"Arial"
fontSize:22];
lblTotalScore.position = ccp(winSize.width * 0.1, winSize.height *
0.35);
[self addChild:lblTotalScore];
```

Notice that we've used the `winSize` variable for positioning. This is useful because it not only keeps things in a relative position on the screen but also helps when coding for multiple devices that have different screen sizes (for example, iPhone 4, iPhone 5, iPad, and so on have different dimensions).

Another way to handle this would be to set the `positionType` of our labels to `CCPositionTypeNormalized`. Then we can set our position values anywhere from 0 to 1, 0 being the far left (or bottom) of the screen, and 1 being the far right (or top) of the screen.

Let's get some text displayed – CCLabelBMFont

If you aren't already familiar, let's recall: BMFonts are the nice, stylized fonts that give your game that extra level of polish without requiring too much effort from you. Refer to *Chapter 6, Tidying Up and Polishing*, to improve the aesthetics of your game. To create BMFont, you have to use a BMFont creator. We're going to use Glyph Designer, as mentioned in *Chapter 1, Refreshing Our Cocos2d Knowledge*.

If you followed the preceding TTF section, then you can just comment out or remove those lines of code, since we are going to redo those fonts and make them BMFont labels in this section.

The first thing we're going to do is create the fonts on the left side of our scene. With Glyph Designer open, select a font from the left panel (I chose **Britannic Bold**, the font in the mock-up). You can mess around with the settings on the right to get a font suitable for your project, but remember that this is only a prototype and you shouldn't spend too much time on it. Have a look at the following screenshot:

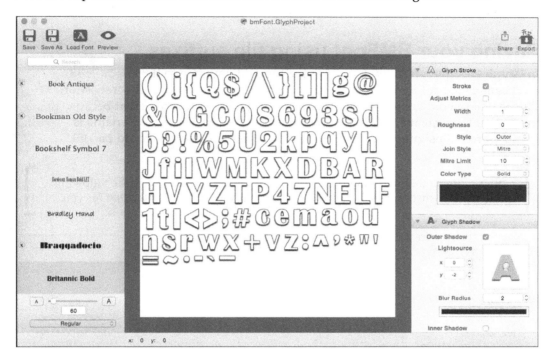

Ensure the font size isn't too big or too small. As you can see in the preceding screenshot, it's set to 60. This is a decent size for the project. If it ends up being too big or too small, adjusting it is fairly simple.

When you're satisfied with the settings you have chosen, click on **Save As** at the top, and select where you want to save the Glyph Designer file (not the actual font file). Now that it has been saved for later use if we decide to edit the font, let's move on to exporting the font so that we can use it in Cocos2d.

Depending on which style of file reading you decided to go with, there are two different ways you'll need to export the font. Make sure you follow the same style as you can use only one of the styles (but not both) within the same project. No matter which route you go by, start with the largest font size you'll need; for example, the preceding screenshot shows a font size of 60 because it's going to be seen on a Retina iPad. If it were only on an iPhone, 60 would be too large.

Saving your BMFont using file suffixes

In Glyph Designer, click on **Export** at the top and navigate to the `Resources/Published-iOS` folder in your project directory (see the following screenshot). This is where you'll export the font for use with Cocos2d. Notice that because this is the largest font, meant for Retina-sized iPads, the suffix after the filename is `-ipadhd`. If you weren't designing for iPad, your largest filename suffix would be `-hd`.

 Note that you should leave the `.fnt/.png` extension (see the following screenshot) as it is. Glyph Designer will automatically add that for you.

Once you've exported the largest phone, go ahead and adjust the settings for each tier you need. For example, since we're exporting -ipadhd at the 60-point font, we'd also want to make 30-point and 15-point sizes for smaller devices. In addition to reducing the font size, we can also modify the stroke and shadow settings to give relatively the same look for all sizes.

So overall, if you call your font bmFont, you should have the following files (each .fnt file will also have a .png file with it), with the largest font size being 60:

- bmFont-ipadhd.fnt - 60-pt

- bmFont-ipad.fnt - 30-pt

- bmFont-hd.fnt - 30-pt

- bmFont.fnt - 15-pt

When using the file extension method, as long as you export your files to the Published-iOS folder, the Xcode project remains set up in a way that includes your fonts in the project. In this way, you don't need to worry about copying anything. That being said, let's begin displaying labels with this new font we just created.

Saving your BMFont using directories

If you chose to go with directories, it's not as simple as just dragging the font files into SpriteBuilder (at the time of writing this book). Instead, you must create four folders within the `Published-iOS` folder of your project directory:

- `resources-phone`
- `resources-phonehd`
- `resources-tablet`
- `resources-tablethd`

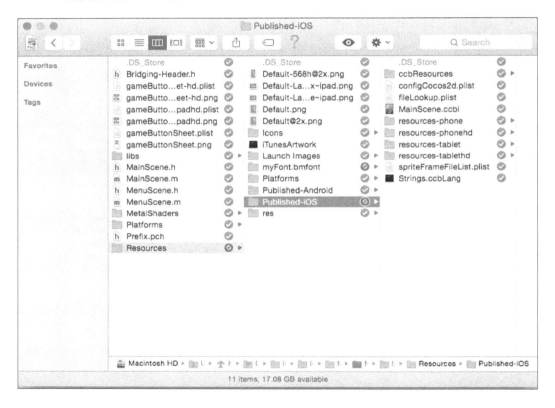

In Glyph Designer, click on **Export** at the top and navigate to the `Published-iOS/resources-tablethd` folder in your project directory (see the following screenshot). This is where you'll export the font for use with Cocos2d. The name of the file here is going to be the name of the font.

Leave the .fnt/.png extension as it is (see the following screenshot). Glyph Designer will automatically add it for you.

Once the `tablethd` version has been exported, do the same export but modify the font size and any other settings you wish to modify. For example, since we're exporting the `tablethd` size at 60-point font, we'd also want to create 30-point and 15-point sizes for smaller devices. In addition to reducing the font size, we can also modify the stroke and shadow settings to give relatively the same look for all sizes.

So overall, if you call your font `bmFont`, you should have the following files (each `.fnt` file will also have a `.png` file with it), with the largest font size being 60:

- `resources-tablethd/bmFont.fnt - 60-pt`

- `resources-tablet/bmFont.fnt - 30-pt`

- `resources-phonehd/bmFont.fnt - 30-pt`

- `resources-phone/bmFont.fnt - 15-pt`

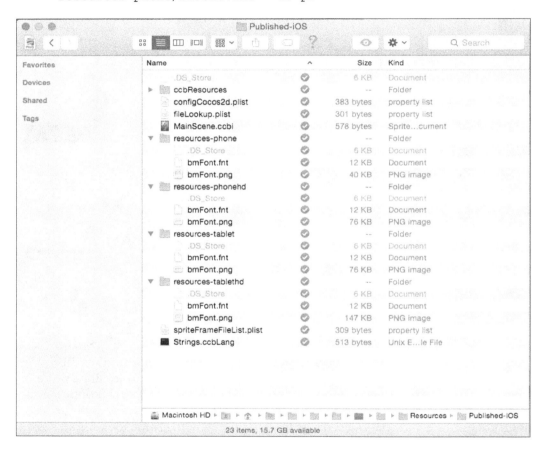

When using the directory method, if you've exported the font files to the folders mentioned previously, the Xcode project will be set up in such a way that it will automatically include these files, so you don't need to worry about copying anything. That being said, let's begin to display labels with this new font we just created.

Exporting the BMFont and importing to Xcode

Bring up Xcode and open `MainScene.h`. You're going to add these variables below the line that says `CGSize winSize`. Again, if you've followed the preceding TTF tutorial, you can delete or comment out the variables we created in that tutorial, as we will be using the same variable names here. We're stating the variable with `lbl` again so that we can easily identify it as a label:

```
@interface MainScene : CCNode
{
  CGSize winSize;
//the labels used for displaying the game info
//this line now uses CCLabelBMFont instead of CCLabelTTFFont
CCLabelBMFont *lblTurnsSurvived, *lblUnitsKilled, *lblTotalScore;
}
```

Then open `MainScene.m` and add these lines of code below the code for the background layer to display the labels. If you had chosen to export your font with a different name, you must change the `fntFile` parameter to match whatever you chose:

```
CCLabelBMFont *lblTurnsSurvivedDesc = [CCLabelBMFont
labelWithString:@"Turns Survived:" fntFile:@"bmFont.fnt"];
lblTurnsSurvivedDesc.position = ccp(winSize.width * 0.125,
winSize.height * 0.8);
[self addChild:lblTurnsSurvivedDesc];

lblTurnsSurvived = [CCLabelBMFont labelWithString:@"0"
fntFile:@"bmFont.fnt"];
lblTurnsSurvived.position = ccp(winSize.width * 0.125,
winSize.height * 0.75);
[self addChild:lblTurnsSurvived];

CCLabelBMFont *lblUnitsKilledDesc = [CCLabelBMFont
labelWithString:@"Units Killed:" fntFile:@"bmFont.fnt"];
lblUnitsKilledDesc.position = ccp(winSize.width * 0.125,
winSize.height * 0.6);
[self addChild:lblUnitsKilledDesc];

lblUnitsKilled = [CCLabelBMFont labelWithString:@"0"
fntFile:@"bmFont.fnt"];
lblUnitsKilled.position = ccp(winSize.width * 0.125,
winSize.height * 0.55);
[self addChild:lblUnitsKilled];
```

```
CCLabelBMFont *lblTotalScoreDesc = [CCLabelBMFont
labelWithString:@"Total Score:" fntFile:@"bmFont.fnt"];
lblTotalScoreDesc.position = ccp(winSize.width * 0.125,
winSize.height * 0.4);
[self addChild:lblTotalScoreDesc];

lblTotalScore = [CCLabelBMFont labelWithString:@"1"
fntFile:@"bmFont.fnt"];
lblTotalScore.position = ccp(winSize.width * 0.125, winSize.height
* 0.35);
[self addChild:lblTotalScore];
```

With these lines added, you should be able to run the game and see some fancy-looking labels on the left side of the screen, as shown here (this was run on an iPhone 5):

It's not much of a game if it's just displaying text, so let's add some buttons. But first, we must go over how to create sprite sheets using TexturePacker.

If you decide not to use TexturePacker, read the *Not using TexturePacker – A brief how-to* section and feel free to skip over the section about using sprite sheets with TexturePacker. If that's the case, you should also be using the directory method of file reading, as there's almost no benefit of file extensions except when using a program that automatically maintains them, such as TexturePacker.

Not using TexturePacker – A brief how-to

As mentioned earlier, if you opt against using TexturePacker, any time it's mentioned to add the image to the sprite sheet, that's your queue to add it to SpriteBuilder and republish it, as it's assumed that you'll be using the directory mode of file reading.

To do this, drag the iPad-retina-sized image into SpriteBuilder, and click on **Publish**. SpriteBuilder will auto-scale.

 Note, however, that in the later chapters of this book, the sprite sheets will be provided (as well as the individual images if you want to do it yourself).

Begin using sprite sheets with TexturePacker

Sprite sheets are used to improve the performance of your game, not only reducing the time it takes for the game to load but also improving the performance while the game is running.

 Unfortunately, TexturePacker works with Cocos2d at the time of writing this book, but its use is not supported by SpriteBuilder directly. However, TexturePacker is a great solution when it comes to building sprite sheets effectively. If you wish to use TexturePacker but are currently using the directory method (the default for SpriteBuilder at the time of writing this book), go back and change your style to file extensions.

As mentioned in *Chapter 1, Refreshing Our Cocos2d Knowledge*, we will be using TexturePacker as the go-to for our sprite sheet creator. TexturePacker is nice for a few reasons:

- It allows exporting to Cocos2d with one click
- It has auto-scaling (up or down) that supports all resolution types
- It makes updating your images later easier to import the images

First, open TexturePacker. Then go to the `Images Pre-Chapter 6` folder, where you'll see the `btnMenu.png` image (our menu button image). Drag it into the right column of TexturePacker. It should look something like this:

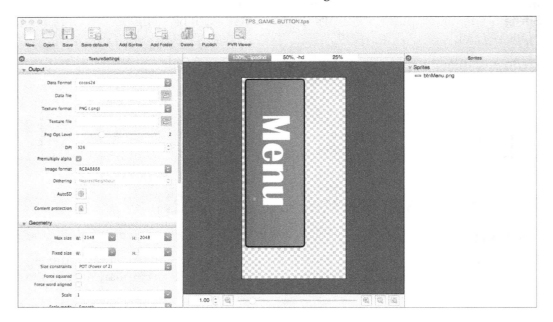

Before changing any of the file locations, make sure you do the following:

1. In the **Texture format** drop-down box, ensure that **PNG** is selected. This format should be fine for most games you'll make. However, if you find yourself wanting to make your game's final project size smaller without sacrificing quality, a recommendation is to switch to **zlib pvr.ccz compression**. This is the most optimal format for Cocos2d, for not only compression per pixel but also performance when drawing the images on the screen.

2. Check the box that says **Premultiply Alpha**. It's not entirely important to know the details of how this works. For now, just know that in Cocos2d, the texture can be rendered faster with this checked.

Saving to the project location

Now that we have the image in TexturePacker, let's modify some of the settings to make sure we can effectively manage any future versions of this sprite sheet. Click on the little folder icon next to the **Data file** textbox and go to the project's `Resources/Published-iOS` directory. Feel free to name the file whatever you want, but try to keep it relevant. For this example, we'll call it `buttonSheet` because it will be the sprite sheet that contains all the buttons in the game. Click on **Save** when you're ready.

 Note that even though the file is being called `buttonSheet.plist`, there is {v} at the end of the filename. This is important, and is what allows TexturePacker to do the auto-scaling for us.

As for image format, it's generally okay to keep it at **RGBA8888**. However, if your game has a large number of art assets on the screen and is suffering performance-wise, changing this to a lower setting might help.

Scaling the images and publishing the sprite sheet

Now we need to make sure TexturePacker will correctly scale what we need. Click on the gear icon next to **AutoSD**, and then open the drop-down box at the top labeled **Presets**. Choose the option that best suits your needs and click on **Apply**.

 If you're only making an iPhone game (and not an iPad version), select **cocos2d hd/sd**.

Otherwise (if you are making an iPad version, which this book's project is), select **cocos2d ipad/hd/sd**.

Finally, in the top-left corner of the screen, we click on the **Save defaults** button, as it allows us to save these settings for any time when we need to create a TexturePacker sprite sheet again. Then click on **Save** (or press *command + S*). This will ask you where you want to the save the TexturePacker file (not the sprite sheet). Generally, you'll save this file in the same folder as all your other art assets. For example, we'll have a separate directory for both the project and the individual art assets that will be copied later.

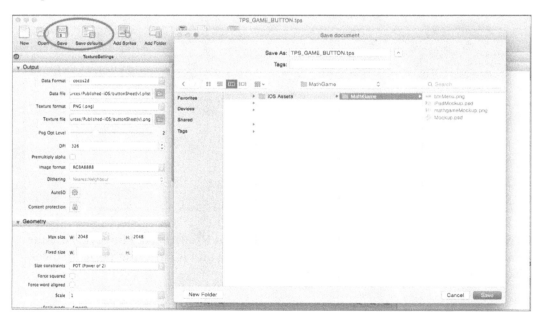

Once you've saved the TPS file in your location of choice, go ahead and click on **Publish**. Publishing will generate the required sprite sheets for the project based on the various settings we entered earlier.

Importing the sprite sheet and loading it into the memory

Finally, once you have published the sprite sheet in the project directory (or anywhere really, but it's best if it's located in the project directory for easy updating later on), the way the Xcode project is set up should cause them to be automatically added to your project.

Once you've published the sprite sheet, open Xcode and go to `AppDelegate.m`. Add one line of code right above the return statement in the `startScene` method to make it look something like this:

```
- (CCScene*) startScene
{

    [[CCSpriteFrameCache sharedSpriteFrameCache]
addSpriteFramesWithFile:@"buttonSheet.plist"];

    return [MainScene scene];//[CCBReader loadAsScene:@"MainScene"];
}
```

Now you're ready to start using the sprite sheet. It took a little bit of work to set it up, but for now, all you need to do is add images to the TexturePacker file, click on **Save**, and then click on Publish. Your changes will be automatically reflected the next time you run your project. That being said, let's make use of the sprite sheet by turning that menu button image into an actual button.

Creating buttons via CCButton and CCLayout

Cocos2d 3.0 changed the way buttons are displayed. If you've used previous versions of Cocos2d, you're probably familiar with CCMenu. That is no longer the way to create and display tappable buttons in Cocos2d. Instead, we're going to use CCButton and place them in a node of the CCLayout type. If you skipped the sprite sheet section, I strongly recommend that you go back and read it. It will save you from many frustrating moments as the project progresses.

For the book's project, we'll be adding the menu button in the bottom-left corner. Like I said, it's extremely easy to add the buttons once you have the images included in the project.

Open the `MainScene.m` file, and add these lines of code below the code for the labels in the `init` method:

```
CCButton *btnMenu = [CCButton buttonWithTitle:@""
    spriteFrame:[CCSpriteFrame frameWithImageNamed:@"btnMenu.png"]];
btnMenu.position = ccp(winSize.width * 0.125, winSize.height *
0.1);
[self addChild:btnMenu];
```

When you run it, you should see the menu button appear in the bottom-left corner. If you used the `pvr.ccz` format and the button flips horizontally, don't worry. Just go back to TexturePacker, check the box that says **Flip PVR**, save the file, and then publish. Go back to Xcode and rerun the project. It should look something like this:

Adding the Restart button

Add the **Restart** button (in this case, `btnRestart.png`) to either TexturePacker or SpriteBuilder depending on which method you used, click on Save, and then publish to update the files so that the **Restart** button can be used. With the **Restart** button's image added, you can modify the `MainScene.m` file's code to look something like this:

```
CCButton *btnMenu = [CCButton buttonWithTitle:@""
spriteFrame:[CCSpriteFrame frameWithImageNamed:@"btnMenu.png"]];
```

```
CCButton *btnRestart = [CCButton buttonWithTitle:@""
spriteFrame:[CCSpriteFrame frameWithImageNamed:@"btnRestart.png"]];

CCLayoutBox *layoutButtons = [[CCLayoutBox alloc] init];
[layoutButtons addChild:btnRestart];
[layoutButtons addChild:btnMenu];
layoutButtons.spacing = 10.f;
layoutButtons.anchorPoint = ccp(0.5f, 0.5f);
layoutButtons.direction = CCLayoutBoxDirectionVertical;
[layoutButtons layout];
layoutButtons.position = ccp(winSize.width * 0.125, winSize.height
* 0.15);
[self addChild:layoutButtons];
```

This will allow the restart button and the menu button to be lined up perfectly. Plus, if you ever decide to move both buttons, but you want them at the same distance relative to each other, just reposition the layout box. And voilà!

What you can do as a quick learning experience is to try messing around with the spacing values; or change the direction, or even the anchor point. You'll get a better understanding of why each line of code is absolutely necessary to create this effect when you try testing different values.

Go ahead and modify some of the values. You can always revert to the preceding code.

So far, using the initial code that you just saw, if you run the project, this is what it will look like:

Creating nodes and units (sprites)

Remember, everything in Cocos2d is, at its base, a CCNode object. Nodes can have other nodes as children. For example, if you wish to create a character with a jetpack attached, the character can be a CCSprite object (a node object with an image) and the jetpack can be a CCSprite object as a child of the character.

Anyway, this is a chapter about prototypes, and we've yet to create any real gameplay. Let's get that going with a few images, some touch controls, and much more.

Setting up the background

Add the background image to the sprite sheet (or SpriteBuilder), save, publish, and then in the MainScene.m file's init method, add the image to the screen as a CCSprite object below the CCLayoutBox code:

```
CCSprite *board = [CCSprite spriteWithImageNamed:@"imgBoard.png"];
board.position = ccp(winSize.width * 0.625, winSize.height/2);
[self addChild:board];
```

Let's run the game, and uh oh! We seem to have run into the first issue with our prototype. Although it's not entirely necessary to get all the bugs and kinks out during this phase, this one is important for the gameplay. Plus, it's a great opportunity to learn about device-specific scaling. If you'll take a look at the following screenshots, one of which was taken on an iPhone 5 and the other on an iPad Retina, you'll notice an issue with the game board being a bit too big on the phone. Here is a screenshot of the game from an iPhone 5:

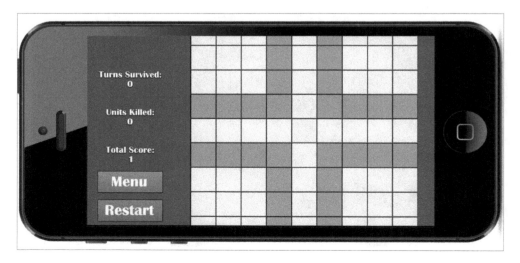

An iPad Retina screenshot of the game appears as follows:

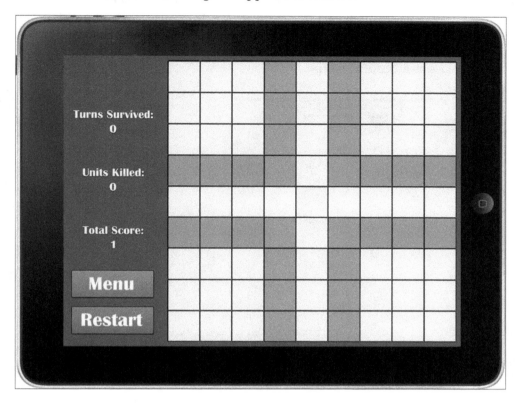

Luckily, it's not too far off, as the auto-scaling from either TexturePacker or SpriteBuilder has given us a relatively accurate scale for the game board. The only thing we need to do is modify the scale of the board very slightly on only the phone, and not the tablet. This can be done by adding these lines of code after you've declared the board variable:

```
if (UI_USER_INTERFACE_IDIOM() == UIUserInterfaceIdiomPhone)
   board.scale = 0.8;
```

Conversely, if you wish to detect an iPad, just use `UIUserInterfaceIdiomPad` instead.

Now, if you run it on a phone (whether it's your own or the simulator), you'll see that the grid is nicely within the screen's bounds.

Defining and adding a unit to the screen

Since each unit is basically the same, except with a different color and number, we should define ourselves a class. To do that, we follow the same instructions regarding a new scene, except that this time, we're going to call the Unit class and set the subclass as a CCSprite type.

Open Unit.h, and make it look like the following:

```objectivec
#import "CCSprite.h"

NS_ENUM(NSInteger, UnitDirection)
{
    DirUp,
    DirDown,
    DirLeft,
    DirRight,
    DirStanding //for when a new one spawns at the center
};

@interface Unit : CCSprite

@property (nonatomic, assign) NSInteger unitValue;
@property (nonatomic, assign) BOOL isFriendly;
@property (nonatomic, assign) enum UnitDirection direction;
//9x9 grid, 1,1 is top left, 9,9 is bottom right
```

```
@property (nonatomic, assign) CGPoint gridPos;
@property (nonatomic, strong) CCColor *color;
@property (nonatomic, strong) CCLabelBMFont *lblValue;

+(Unit*)friendlyUnit;
+(Unit*)enemyUnitWithNumber:(NSInteger)value atGridPosition:(CGPoint)
pos;
@end
```

This will basically allow us to give our units a move direction. We also get a value associated with them, a Boolean to determine whether it's a friendly unit or not (needed for both movement as well as collisions), and various other stuff.

Now open Unit.m and add the following code between @implementation and @end:

```
+(Unit*)friendlyUnit
{
  return [[self alloc] initWithFriendlyUnit];
}


+(Unit*)enemyUnitWithNumber:(NSInteger)num
atGridPosition:(CGPoint)pos
{
  return [[self alloc] initWithEnemyWithNumber:num atPos:pos];
}


-(id)initCommon
{
  if ((self=[super initWithImageNamed:@"imgUnit.png"]))
  {
    if (UI_USER_INTERFACE_IDIOM() == UIUserInterfaceIdiomPhone)
      self.scale = 0.8;

    self.lblValue = [CCLabelBMFont labelWithString:@"1"
fntFile:@"bmFont.fnt"];
    self.lblValue.scale = 1.5;
    self.lblValue.position = ccp(self.contentSize.width/2,
self.contentSize.height/1.75);
    [self addChild:self.lblValue];
  }
  return self;
}
```

```objc
-(id)initWithFriendlyUnit
{
  if ((self=[self initCommon]))
  {
    self.isFriendly = YES;
    self.unitValue = 1;
    self.direction = DirStanding;
    self.color = [CCColor colorWithRed:0 green:0.8f blue:0];
//green for friendly
    self.gridPos = ccp(5,5);
  }
  return self;
}

-(id)initWithEnemyWithNumber:(NSInteger)num atPos:(CGPoint)p
{
  if ((self=[self initCommon]))
  {
    self.isFriendly = NO;
    self.unitValue = num;
    self.lblValue.string = [NSString stringWithFormat:@"%ld",
(long)num];
    self.direction = DirLeft;
    self.color = [CCColor colorWithRed:0.8f green:0 blue:0]; //red
for enemy
    self.gridPos = p;
  }
  return self;
}
```

The `init` methods set up some important stuff: position on the grid, color, whether it's a friendly unit or not, the value of the unit when it first spawns, the label in which to show the value, and the direction it intends to move on the next turn.

Let's open `MainScene.m` and spawn a friendly unit and an enemy unit on the screen. Because we defined the class so well, it's very simple to spawn two units with only a few lines of code. Make sure you include the `Unit.h` at the top too:

```objc
Unit *friendly = [Unit friendlyUnit];
friendly.position = ccp(winSize.width/2, winSize.height/2);
[self addChild:friendly];

Unit *enemy = [Unit enemyUnitWithNumber:1
atGridPosition:ccp(1,1)];
```

```
enemy.position = ccp(winSize.width - 50, winSize.height/2);
[self addChild:enemy];
```

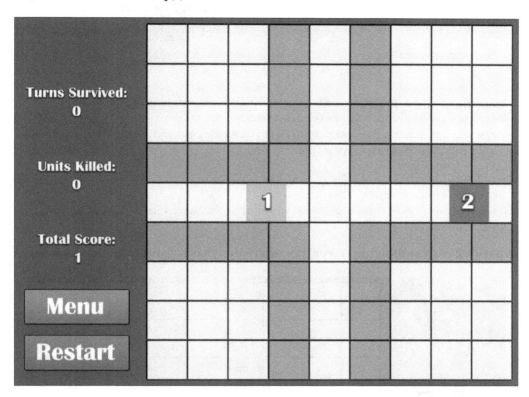

However, the positions still need to be calculated, and the fact that we assigned a grid coordinate doesn't mean anything to the game. We need to determine the actual positions on the screen. That is, if we say the position is (5, 5), it better know that means smack dab in the middle of the grid. However, the only place that knows the screen coordinates is the main scene, so open MainScene.m and add the following method to get the screen position based on a grid coordinate:

```
-(CGPoint)getPositionForGridCoord:(CGPoint)pos
{
  CGPoint screenPos;
  Unit *u = [Unit friendlyUnit];

  CGFloat borderValue = 1.f;
  if (UI_USER_INTERFACE_IDIOM() == UIUserInterfaceIdiomPhone)
    borderValue = 0.6f;
```

```
   screenPos.x = winSize.width * 0.625 + (u.boundingBox.size.width
+ borderValue) * (pos.x-5);
   screenPos.y = winSize.height/2 - (u.boundingBox.size.width +
borderValue) * (pos.y-5);

   return screenPos;
}
```

```
Now change the positioning of the units to reflect this change:
Unit *friendly = [Unit friendlyUnit];
friendly.position = [self getPositionForGridCoord:friendly.gridPos];
[self addChild:friendly];

Unit *enemy = [Unit enemyUnitWithNumber:2
atGridPosition:ccp(4,7)];
enemy.position = [self getPositionForGridCoord:enemy.gridPos];
[self addChild:enemy];
```

Have a look at the following screenshot; this is how your game will now look like:

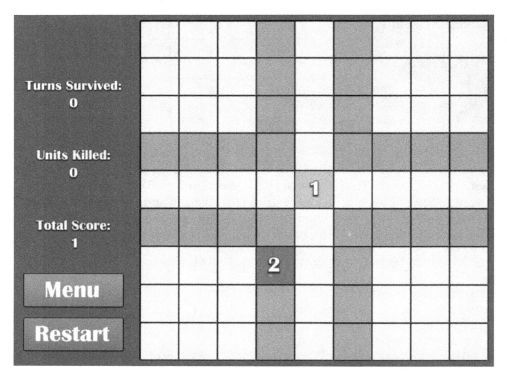

Running the game should get you something like what is shown in the preceding screenshot. And yes, even though this screenshot is from an iPad, the code works equally well on an iPhone of any resolution, as the formula for determining the position works on the assumption that (5, 5) is the center of the grid.

Now let's get these units moving around the screen with some touch mechanics. First, place the red unit to the right of the green in the rightmost section of the grid—(9, 5), for those who are lazy and don't want to calculate it.

Moving the units around with touch controls

Touch detection is extremely easy in Cocos2d. From version 3.3 onwards, all you need to do is add one line of code and a few methods, and you're good.

That being said, add this line of code to the `initWithFriendlyUnit` method of the `Unit` class (we want to enable touch only on the friendly units, not the enemies):

```
[self setUserInteractionEnabled:YES];
```

Then add the following methods in Unit.m that will intercept all touches made on each unit:

```
-(void)touchBegan:(CCTouch *)touch withEvent:(CCTouchEvent *)event
{

}

-(void)touchMoved:(CCTouch *)touch withEvent:(CCTouchEvent *)event
{

}

-(void)touchEnded:(CCTouch *)touch withEvent:(CCTouchEvent *)event
{

}
```

These methods are fairly self-descriptive in terms of what they do. The `touchBegan` method registers a touch every time a finger touches the screen, the `touchMoved` method registers a touch every time the finger is dragged along the screen, and the `touchEnded` method registers when the finger is lifted off the screen.

In order to determine which unit is being dragged and in which direction, add these three variables to the Unit.h file:

```
@property (nonatomic, assign) BOOL isBeingDragged;
@property (nonatomic, assign) CGPoint touchDownPos;
@property (nonatomic, assign) enum UnitDirection dragDirection;
```

Also add this method declaration:

```
-(void)updateLabel;
```

Once that's done, open Unit.m and add code to the following methods.

First you must create this method, which will set the displayed string of the Unit's label to the Unit's actual value:

```
-(void)updateLabel
{
    self.lblValue.string = [NSString stringWithFormat:@"%ld",
(long)self.unitValue];
}
```

Then we need to handle our touches in order to update the label, so the following code needs to be added to the touchBegan method, which will grab the CCTouch method's location relative to where it is inside a given node. For now, we want to know where the touch is occurring relative to the Unit itself, and we'll set that in our touchDownPos variable:

```
self.touchDownPos = [touch locationInNode:self];
self.dragDirection = DirStanding;
```

Then you have to add the following code to the touchMoved method. This will determine what direction the finger is being dragged, based on the x and y difference from touchDownPos and the current touchPos variables:

```
CGPoint touchPos = [touch locationInNode:self];
//if it's not already being dragged and the touch is dragged far
enough away...
if (!self.isBeingDragged && ccpDistance(touchPos,
self.touchDownPos) > 6)
{
    self.isBeingDragged = YES;

    CGPoint difference = ccp(touchPos.x - self.touchDownPos.x,
touchPos.y - self.touchDownPos.y);
    //determine direction
```

```
if (difference.x > 0)
{
    if (difference.x > fabsf(difference.y))
      self.dragDirection = DirRight;
    else if (difference.y > 0)
      self.dragDirection = DirUp;
    else
      self.dragDirection = DirDown;
}
else
{
    if (difference.x < -1* fabsf(difference.y))
      self.dragDirection = DirLeft;
    else if (difference.y > 0)
      self.dragDirection = DirUp;
    else
      self.dragDirection = DirDown;
}
}
```

Finally, add this section of code to the `touchEnded` method. This will actually update the grid position of the unit based on what direction it was being dragged in:

```
//if it was being dragged in the first place
if (self.isBeingDragged)
{
  CGPoint touchPos = [touch locationInNode:self];
  //stop the dragging
  self.isBeingDragged = NO;

  if (ccpDistance(touchPos, self.touchDownPos) >
self.boundingBox.size.width/2)
    {
        NSInteger gridX, gridY;
        gridX = self.gridPos.x;
        gridY = self.gridPos.y;

        //move unit that direction
        if (self.dragDirection == DirUp)
          --gridY;
        else if (self.dragDirection == DirDown)
          ++gridY;
        else if (self.dragDirection == DirLeft)
          --gridX;
```

```
        else if (self.dragDirection == DirRight)
          ++gridX;

        //keep within the grid bounds
        if (gridX < 1) gridX = 1;
        if (gridY > 9) gridX = 9;

        if (gridY < 1) gridY = 1;
        if (gridY > 9) gridY = 9;

        //if it's not in the same place... aka, a valid move taken
        if (!(gridX == self.gridPos.x && gridY == self.gridPos.y))
        {
          self.gridPos = ccp(gridX, gridY);
          self.unitValue++;
          self.direction = self.dragDirection;
          [self updateLabel];
        }
      }
    }
```

Now, if you run the game, you'll see that when you tap (or click, if running on the simulator) and drag that unit... oh my! Why isn't the unit moving? We set the grid coordinate and everything! Even the unit's value is being increased properly.

But aye! We didn't tell the main scene that the unit needed to be moved, since that's where the unit positioning happens. That being said, we want a way to let our main scene know that a unit was moved so that we can update its position.

Talking between scenes

A very common way to do this is by making use of NSNotificationCenter. It's broken down into two parts: a sender and a receiver. The sender is called a notification and the receiver is called an observer. What we need to do is send a notification through NSNotificationCenter so that any observer set up can receive the notification.

First, we need to declare a constant to reduce human errors when coding. We want to do this because the notifications need to be exact, or else they won't work.

So, open Unit.h and add this line below #import but above NS_ENUM:

```
FOUNDATION_EXPORT NSString *const kTurnCompletedNotification;
```

Then, at the top of Unit.m, below the #import statement but above @implementation, insert this line of code:

```
NSString *const kTurnCompletedNotification = @"unitDragComplete";
```

It doesn't entirely matter what the string is; it's just that it has to be something unique from any other notification you end up creating later on.

Then go ahead and add this little line of code right below the [self updateLabel] line in the touchEnded method of Unit.m:

```
//pass the unit through to the MainScene
[[NSNotificationCenter defaultCenter]
postNotificationName:kTurnCompletedNotification object:nil
userInfo:@{@"unit" : self}];
```

This will send a notification to the observer that something has happened. In this case, we want to notify the main scene that the current unit has been moved via dragging and needs its position updated. That's why we pass self (the current Unit)—so that we can update the position of the specific unit that was moved.

Finally, let's hop over to MainScene.m and add the following code at the bottom of (or top of; it's your preference) the init method:

```
[[NSNotificationCenter defaultCenter] addObserver:self
selector:@selector(moveUnit:) name:kTurnCompletedNotification
object:nil];
```

Then add the following methods: moveUnit and dealloc. The moveUnit method is what we want called when the notification gets pushed. We have an NSNotification parameter that grabs the NSDictionary parameter passed from the Unit class. We also need the dealloc to remove the observer, or else it could catch future notifications by accident, and that can cause the game to crash:

```
- (void)moveUnit:(NSNotification*)notif
{
  NSDictionary *userInfo = [notif userInfo];
  Unit *u = (Unit*)userInfo[@"unit"];
  u.position = [self getPositionForGridCoord:u.gridPos];
}

- (void)dealloc
{
  [[NSNotificationCenter defaultCenter] removeObserver:self];
}
```

Hurray! Now when you run the code, you should get the unit shifting from grid spot to grid spot with each swipe, in any direction. Now it's starting to feel like a game. However, it still lacks interaction with the enemies, and none of the scores are being increased. Let's add that next.

Interaction with enemies and scoring

First, we need some variables to keep track of the numbers. So in `MainScene.h`, add this under the BMFont label variables:

```
NSInteger numTurnSurvived, numUnitsKilled, numTotalScore;
```

In `MainScene.m`, add the following method to update the label for each counter:

```
-(void)updateLabels
{
  lblTotalScore.string = [NSString stringWithFormat:@"%ld",
(long)numTotalScore];
  lblTurnsSurvived.string = [NSString stringWithFormat:@"%ld",
(long)numTurnSurvived];
  lblUnitsKilled.string = [NSString stringWithFormat:@"%ld",
(long)numUnitsKilled];
}
```

Add these lines to the `moveUnit` method to increment the respective numbers:

```
++numTurnSurvived;
++numTotalScore;
[self updateLabels];
```

Then initialize the variables somewhere in the `init` method:

```
numTotalScore = 1;
numTurnSurvived = 0;
numUnitsKilled = 0;
```

Now you'll notice that each time your unit moves around, the score and the `turns survived` labels increases by 1. But the unit can still go straight through the enemy unit. Let's fix that.

First, we need to compare the grid locations after a move with all possible enemies on the screen to see whether there was a collision. However, if we're going to cycle through all the enemies, it means we'll need an array to hold them all, so we declare an `NSMutableArray` parameter in the `MainScene.h` file:

```
NSMutableArray *arrEnemies;
```

At the bottom of the `init` method in the `MainScene.m` file, after you spawn the enemy, add the following lines of code:

```
arrEnemies = [[NSMutableArray alloc] init];
[arrEnemies addObject:enemy];
```

At the end of the `moveUnit` method, we need to cycle through all the enemies and check whether the grid location is the same (that is, whether we're about to run into an enemy):

```
//for each Unit in the arrEnemies array...
for (Unit *enemy in arrEnemies)
{
  if (enemy.gridPos.x == u.gridPos.x &&
      enemy.gridPos.y == u.gridPos.y)
  {
     //collision!

  }
}
```

Under the collision comment, we now want to compare the unit values. Whichever unit has the higher value will win, and the unit with the lower value will be removed from the board (and the array). In the case of a tie, both will be removed. It's also important to update the `unitsKilled` counter here:

```
{
      //collision!
      NSInteger enemyVal = enemy.unitValue;
      NSInteger friendVal = u.unitValue;

      //tie, both dead
      if (enemyVal == friendVal)
      {
        [self removeChild:u];
        [arrEnemies removeObject:enemy];
        [self removeChild:enemy];
        ++numUnitsKilled;
      }
      //enemy higher
      else if (enemy.unitValue > u.unitValue)
      {
        enemy.unitValue -= friendVal;
        [enemy updateLabel];
        [self removeChild:u];
      }
      //friendly higher
      else
```

```
    {
      u.unitValue -= enemyVal;
      [u updateLabel];
      [arrEnemies removeObject:enemy];
      [self removeChild:enemy];
      ++numUnitsKilled;
    }

    //exit the for loop so no "bad things" happen
    break;
}
```

Finally, move the [self updateLabels] method call in the moveUnit method to the end of the method (that is, after the loop ends), or else the unitsKilled label won't be updated until the next turn, which might confuse your players.

That's it! You can move around, run into enemies, combine your score, have the labels updated, and even restart the game if you lose (by going to **Menu** and tapping the **Play** button). Here's what the game more or less looks like so far.

On an iPad, the game scene appears as follows:

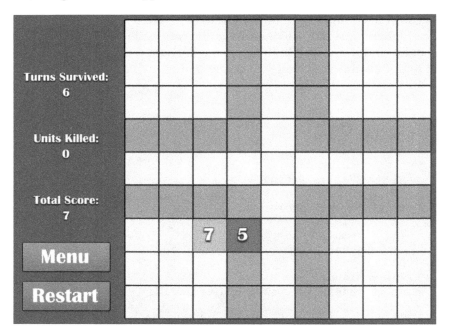

On an iPhone 5, the game scene appears like this:

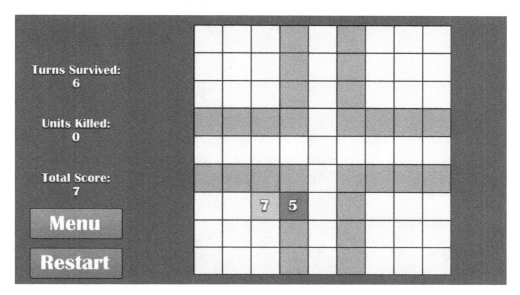

Creating menus, scenes, and scene transitions

Scenes make up the core of Cocos2d. When you go from the main menu to the **Level Select** screen, those are (when done in a best practice coding way) two different scenes. You can transition from one scene to another in any way your heart desires. However, it's generally done by tapping a button. For example, **Play**, **Settings**, and **Shop** are all examples of a menu button that a user might press to trigger a scene transition.

Creating a new file for the scene

Most likely, your game isn't going to have just one screen. If so, then you can skim over this as it likely won't pertain to you. However, the vast majority of games made have at the very least a main menu, a settings menu, a pause screen, and some sort of screen besides the main game screen.

The next few screenshots show how to create a file with a CCNode object as the parent class. If you already know how to do this, feel free to skip to the next step.

In Xcode, right-click (or press *Ctrl* and click) on the source folder at the top of the project navigator, and then click on **New File** as shown in the following screenshot:

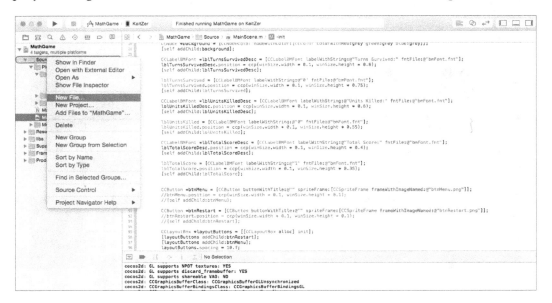

In the dialog window that opens, under the iOS **Source** section, select **Cocoa Touch Class** and click on **Next** as shown in the following screenshot:

Name the class something relevant, as you may have to go back to it later. We're going to use `MenuScene` as the name of our class. Once you've named the class, click on **Next**.

 Make sure you change **Subclass of** to `CCNode`, or else you'll be unable to make a new scene out of it.

Talking about where to save the file, it's recommended to keep all of your project's class files in the same directory. As shown in the following screenshot, we're saving the **MenuScene** file we wish to create in the `Source` folder, where the **MainScene** files are located.

Once you've chosen a location, click on **Create** as shown in the following screenshot:

Turning a class into an official CCScene subclass

It's not officially a scene yet, but that's what we're going to add now. In the header file of the class you just created, add a similar block of code between the `@interface` and `@end` lines—like what we have in the `MainScene.m` file. For example, your header might look something like this:

```
@interface MenuScene : CCNode
{
  CGSize winSize;
}
+(CCScene*)scene;
@end
```

Then, in the main file for the class, add the following between the `@implementation` and `@end` lines (yes, it's a copy-paste job for each scene you create):

```
+(CCScene *)scene
{
  return [[self alloc] init];
}
```

```
-(id)init
{
  if ((self=[super init]))
  {

  }
  return self;
}
```

With that in place, you can now begin to add code to the main menu scene. Let's quickly add a background color to the init method so that we know the scene works when we eventually link a button and transition to it. We're going to give it a random green color, because the default is black:

```
-(id)init
{
  if ((self=[super init]))
  {
    //these values range 0 to 1.0, so use float to get ratio
    CCNode *background = [CCNodeColor nodeWithColor:[CCColor
colorWithRed:58/255.f green:138/255.f blue:88/255.f]];
    [self addChild:background];
  }
  return self;
}
```

Linking the button in the game to go to the menu

Open MainScene.m, and include the scene you created at the top of the file:

```
#import "MainScene.h"
#import "MenuScene.h" //the line to add. Note: it says MENU scene,
not MAIN scene. They're similar, but different. We want both here.

@implementation MainScene
```

Then go to the section of code where you declared the **Menu** button. Right after you declare it, add the following line of code. This will connect the menu button to a method called goToMenu. The setTarget method is the way CCButton knows what to do when it gets tapped:

```
[btnMenu setTarget:self selector:@selector(goToMenu)];
```

Then, below the `init` method, add the `goToMenu` method, like this:

```
-(void)goToMenu
{
    [[CCDirector sharedDirector] replaceScene:[MenuScene scene]];
}
```

With these three things added, you should be able to run the game and click on the menu button. Voilà! We have a transition to the Menu scene, albeit rather ugly at the moment. But there's no way to get back to the game screen, so let's add a **Play** button to do so.

Creating and linking a button in the menu to go to the game

Now that we're able to get to the **Menu** scene, let's quickly add a **Play** button so that we can start to create the core of the gameplay and round out this prototype.

First, add the **Play** button to TexturePacker, save, and publish. Then open `MenuScene.m` and add the following to the `init` method:

```
winSize = [CCDirector sharedDirector].viewSize;
CCButton *btnPlay = [CCButton buttonWithTitle:@""
spriteFrame:[CCSpriteFrame frameWithImageNamed:@"btnPlay.png"]];
btnPlay.position = ccp(winSize.width/2, winSize.height/2);
[btnPlay setTarget:self selector:@selector(goToGame)];
[self addChild:btnPlay];
```

Also add the `goToGame` method below `init` so that the button actually has a method to call:

```
-(void)goToGame
{
    [[CCDirector sharedDirector] replaceScene:[MainScene scene]];
}
```

Run the project and click on the **Menu** button. You should see a clickable **Play** button that will take you back to the game. Yay, scene transitions! Now that the play button is in place and we have the basic layout between scenes, we can get working on the core of the game.

One final thing you could do would be to create a `restartGame` method, set the target of the **Restart** button to `self`, and set the selector of the restart button to the `restartGame` method. Inside the `restartGame` method you have created, simply call the `replaceScene` method (like what you just did), but this time, use `MainScene` instead of `MenuScene` so that the scene transitions to a fresh/clean/new/whatever version of itself. This is a good idea because this is the minimal code for the very effect we're trying to achieve here.

Where to go from here?

It's quite clear that the project is far from complete at this stage. However, there are a lot of things that are a core of the game's implementation: the dragging, the scoring, and the grid formation. From here on, it's probably best to continue to iterate on the project and slowly add stuff until it's a fully working prototype with very minimal baseline mechanics working. For example, we could add some enemy spawning, **Artificial Intelligence** (**AI**), the user's units automatically moving, and so on.

But as far as this book is concerned, we're going to move on as the point of this chapter was to go straight into a prototype. That's basically what we have here — something we can show our friends and family and say, "Hey, this is what the concept is, and this is what I've got so far." With the prototype, you can gauge things such as the following:

- Is the game board too small for the player's fingers?
- Is the concept too confusing?
- Is it hard to interact with the character?

With time, all of these will be sorted, but it's better to learn about the biggest problems early on rather than find them after your game has been published on the App Store and you notice that nobody is downloading it.

Some suggestions

If you're following the book's tutorial/example project (which I hope you are), try adding the following on your own, all of which will be added outside this book for consolidation purposes:

- Automatically moving the red unit each turn and increasing its score
- Spawning a red unit every three or four turns around the border and adding it to the array (and possibly implementing the movement as you did with the previous red unit)

- Spawning another friendly unit with a value of 1 when you move away from (5, 5)

- Creating and maintaining a friendly unit array

- Making all friendly units move in the direction they were last instructed

Don't worry if you don't want to take the time to implement these by yourself. A later chapter will have them pre-implemented, and you can download the source code to get an up-to-date version before you begin that chapter.

However, it is highly recommended that you do try coding on your own, as that's the entire point of this book—to push you further as a coder. The tutorials are here for support, but the main purpose is to show you cool things and let you run loose with the tools at your disposal.

Summary

A prototype for the game, as shown in this chapter, can be done relatively quickly (not that many pages compared to how much content was put in). If you have a large-scale game (which is almost certainly the case), now would be the best time to go about creating the other scenes, adding buttons that link the scenes together, creating the characters in the game, and even adding some baseline code for the core of the game.

In general, the way to prototype quickly and iterate more often is to get the simplest parts that draw a wireframe of the project first so that the people holding the prototype can fill the gaps with their imagination (or if you hand them a near-complete project, they won't have to fill any gaps). It's like drawing a person on a piece of paper. First, you draw a rough version of their body position, then fill in a bit of the muscle and fat, and finally draw the details such as fingers, clothes, facial expressions, and so on.

In the next chapter, we'll cover in depth how to create some really awesome mechanics and do with Cocos2d what most developers don't do.

3
Focusing on Physics

This chapter is for those of you who want to incorporate physics into your games. Whether you're building a mini golf game that uses realistic wall bounces or a platformer with endless gravity, this chapter is for you. It will have tutorials on the physics side of games, as well as show you how to use a physics engine without gravity.

In this chapter, we will cover the following topics:

- How Chipmunk works
- Setting up a project and creating basic objects
- Setting gravity by tilting the device
- Handling collisions in Chipmunk

You must use Chipmunk for collision detection only (and not physics). Not all games need (or should even consider using) a physics engine. Sometimes, it's better to leave it out. However, if you feel your game will either be more polished or be produced faster, then by all means use it. That being said, the project in this book will not need a physics engine. So, instead of following the project here, we will create a small project that has many modular examples that can be adapted in your other projects. The book's main project will continue in the next chapter.

You may have been used to using the Box2D physics engine, but ever since version 3.0 of Cocos2d, there is no longer any support from the developers to make Box2D work out of the box as it did in previous versions. That being said, this chapter will focus on Chipmunk. If this chapter does not cover everything you need as far as physics is concerned, feel free to check out the documentation at `http://chipmunk-physics.net/documentation.php`. It also has a variety of online tutorials.

Learn how Chipmunk works

As previously mentioned, Chipmunk is the physics engine that's integrated with Cocos2d, and is the main physics engine from version 3.0 onwards. The good news for both newcomers and fans of Box2D alike is that Chipmunk is very simple to use. Let's get down to how Chipmunk basically works.

Overall structure of Chipmunk

Chipmunk is a physics engine in Cocos2d that simulates real-world physics, that is, making use of gravity, collisions, objects bouncing off each other, and so on.

Chipmunk uses a "bodies within a world" way of doing things. This means that, as shown in the following diagram, there's a physics simulation happening (called a **world**), and anything with physics applicable to it is a **body**. You just create a world that will simulate physics on the bodies within, and off you go. Each world you create will have its own gravity attached to it.

This is a simple representation of bodies within a world. Note that the entire green rectangle is the world, and the individual squares are bodies within it.

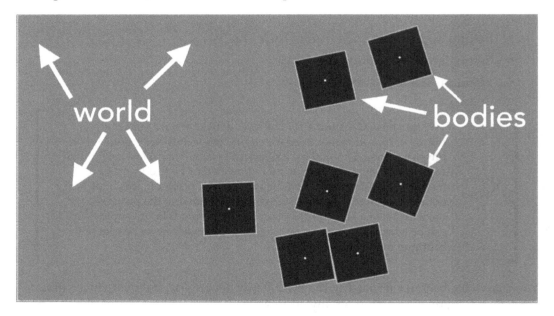

Each body has a type (explained in the next section) as well as properties such as density, mass, friction, elasticity, velocity, and more. In Cocos2d, you can attach a physics body to a sprite with a single line of code, and the sprite will move around to the place where the body is located.

When these objects have their boundaries touching/intersecting one another, it's a collision. When a collision occurs, you can handle it however you wish.

Types of bodies

Chipmunk has three types of physics bodies that can be added to the world. They are static, dynamic, and kinematic:

- **Static bodies**: These are the walls, ground, immovable rocks, and other objects in the game. They will not be affected by any gravity or other forces that try to interact with them.
- **Dynamic bodies**: These are the default when creating a `CCPhysicsBody` object. These are the objects that will go flying around, colliding with other objects, and have forces act upon them.
- **Kinematic bodies**: These are a sort of hybrid body type that cannot be influenced by forces or gravity, but can still be moved by `CCActions` and other methods.

In general, you will only be using static and dynamic bodies (and so is the case with this chapter). If you feel that you need more help with kinematic body types, check out the Cocos2d documentation about physics bodies at `http://www.cocos2d-swift.org/docs/api/Constants/CCPhysicsBodyType.html`.

Now that you know how Chipmunk works from a technical perspective, let's actually get down to the coding so that we can see these physics bodies for ourselves.

Setting up a project and creating basic objects

The Chipmunk physics engine is fairly well integrated within the Cocos2d library. It works within SpriteBuilder as well as programmatically within Cocos2d. As with the rest of this book, we will be focusing on creating the project with code, and only using SpriteBuilder as the tool for project creation. So, create a new project in SpriteBuilder and publish it. If you've forgotten how to do this, feel free to go back and reference the project creation in the first chapter.

Setting up Cocos2d for use with physics

First, we need to lay down the groundwork so that we can begin to code with it, as the published SpriteBuilder project uses the SpriteBuilder files and not the actual coded scenes. Similar to the previous chapter, open `AppDelegate.m` and add the following line of code to the top of the file:

```
#import "MainScene.h"
```

Then, in the `startScene` method of the `AppDelegate.m` file, replace that one line of code that already exists with the following:

```
return [MainScene scene];
```

With that in place, open `MainScene.h` and add code such that your file looks something like this (make sure you change the `CCNode` inheritance to `CCScene`, or else some later methods won't work):

```
@interface MainScene : CCScene {
  CGSize winSize;
}
+(CCScene*)scene;
@end
```

Finally, open `MainScene.m` and add this block of code between the `@implementation` and `@end` lines:

```
+(CCScene*)scene
{
  return [[self alloc] init];
}

-(id)init
{
  if ((self=[super init]))
  {
    winSize = [[CCDirector sharedDirector] viewSize];

    //these values range 0 to 1.0, so use float to get ratio
    CCNode *background = [CCNodeColor nodeWithColor:[CCColor
colorWithRed:58/255.f green:138/255.f blue:88/255.f]];
    [self addChild:background];
  }
  return self;
}
```

If you run the project at this point (in any simulator or on any device), you'll see a full, green screen. If you don't, go back and make sure you copy all of the code as instructed. If you do see the green color, then you're set to move on to the next section.

Building a world for physics to exist

Cocos2d is simply a graphics engine, and we need to create a Chipmunk physics simulation environment so that we can make use of the library. This sounds a lot more complicated than it actually is. Basically, we create a CCPhysicsNode object, and then add our sprites and nodes to this object, instead of self.

 Remember, self is a reference to the current object. In the past, we've added objects to the screen using [self addChild:], but with the CCPhysicsNode object, we're going to add objects using [world addChild:], since world will be the name of our CCPhysicsNode object.

So, open MainScene.h and add the declaration for the world variable below the winSize declaration:

```
CCPhysicsNode *world;
```

Then open MainScene.m and add this block of code after the background is created in the init method:

```
//create the physics simulation world
world = [CCPhysicsNode node];
world.debugDraw = YES;
world.gravity = ccp(0, -300);
[self addChild:world];
```

And that's it! The preceding code will create a physics world that allows physics to be simulated. All we need to do next is create some CCNode objects, add physics bodies to the CCNode objects, then add the CCNode objects to the physics world (instead of self).

 Downloading the example code

You can download the example code files from your account at http://www.packtpub.com for all the Packt Publishing books you have purchased. If you purchased this book elsewhere, you can visit http://www.packtpub.com/support and register to have the files e-mailed directly to you.

Setting `debugDraw` to `YES` ensures that whenever we attach any physics body to a `CCNode` object and add it to the world, we will have an outline of that body's shape drawn over our objects. Thus, we will know exactly where each body is and how it's colliding. Normally, when `debugDraw` is not turned on, we won't see these shapes.

The collision will still work the same whether you have `debugDraw` on or not. The main purpose is to, well, debug the project to make sure the physics bodies are added and colliding as intended.

Enabling touch creation of our object

Now we are going to need some objects on the screen that we want to collide with one another. Instead of programmatically spawning the objects, let's have the objects spawn wherever the user touches the screen.

So, open `MainScene.m` and add the following line of code anywhere in the `init` method. This will allow you to grab any touch data from the user:

```
[self setUserInteractionEnabled:YES];
```

Then, below the `init` method, we add this method so that we can start receiving touches in our scene. This method (as seen in the previous chapter) will grab any touch event, and we want to grab the location of the touch so that we can position the object accordingly. Then we will spawn a black square at the touch position:

```
- (void)touchBegan:(CCTouch *)touch withEvent:(CCTouchEvent *)event
{
    CGPoint touchPos = [touch locationInNode:self];
    //create a black square
    CGFloat width = winSize.width * 0.1f;
    CCNode *square = [CCNodeColor nodeWithColor:[CCColor colorWithRed:0
    green:0 blue:0] width:width height:width];
    square.position = touchPos;
    square.anchorPoint = ccp(0.5f,0.5f);
    [world addChild:square];
}
```

This will create a node that's 10 percent of the screen's width and add it to the `world` object. We're adding it to `world` instead of `self` because when we add physics bodies to the square, we want the simulation to handle the object's movement. We need to set the `anchorPoint` of the node because, by default, a `CCNode` has its anchor point at (0,0).

If you run the game at this point, you will see the same green screen. As you tap around the screen, black squares will appear, centered at the touch location.

However, you'll notice that even though we've added them to the world object, they aren't falling according to the gravity we set up, and they aren't colliding and pushing each other around. What we have to do next is create a CCPhysicsBody object and assign it to the created square so that the physics simulation will handle the movement properly.

> If you're still a bit unsure what exactly CCPhysicsBody is, it's essentially an object that has a shape, or perimeter, that defines where the object can collide with other objects. CCPhysicsBody also has other properties such as elasticity, restitution, density, and so on, and is best used when attached to a CCNode object so that the node can have its movement handled by the physics body.

Making the objects fall – adding CCPhysicsBody

In the MainScene.m file, add the following code to the bottom of the touchBegan method. This will add the physics body we want to the square:

```
//add a physics body to the black square
CCPhysicsBody *squareBody = [CCPhysicsBody
bodyWithRect:CGRectMake(0, 0, width, width) cornerRadius:0];
squareBody.elasticity = 0.5f;
square.physicsBody = squareBody;
```

With this code in place, when you run the game, you will notice that the objects not only begin to fall but also have that debug square that was mentioned earlier. Notice that we don't have to declare the body type as **dynamic**, as that's the default. Also note the **elasticity** (which, as you might recall, is the bounciness) of 0.5. This is set so that the squares don't go bouncing all over the place. If we wanted that, we would've set the elasticity to a higher number, such as 1.0.

But oh no! The squares just fall off the screen as if it's a bottomless pit. Let's fix that.

Adding the ground and walls

Creating a ground object is easy, but since the walls and the ceiling are basically the same thing, let's define a method that will take in CGRect and create for us a static, invisible node with those dimensions.

So, anywhere in MainScene.m, add the following method:

```
- (void) addWallWithRect: (CGRect) rect
{
  CCPhysicsBody *wallBody = [CCPhysicsBody bodyWithRect:rect
cornerRadius:0];
  wallBody.type = CCPhysicsBodyTypeStatic;
  wallBody.elasticity = .5f;

  CCNode *wall = [CCNode node];
  wall.physicsBody = wallBody;
  [world addChild:wall];
}
```

This code is fairly similar to the square's code, except for one notable difference: the type of the physics body. We set it to static because we don't want the gravity affecting it, nor do we want the squares to push the ground in any direction.

Just because we declared a method doesn't mean it will automatically generate walls for us. So, go to your init method and add the following block of code to add the walls around the edges of the device:

```
/***** Add Ground, Walls, and Ceiling *****/

//ground
[self addWallWithRect:CGRectMake(0, 0, winSize.width, 1)];

//left wall
[self addWallWithRect:CGRectMake(0, 0, 1, winSize.height)];

//right wall
[self addWallWithRect:CGRectMake(winSize.width, 0, 1, winSize.
height)];

//ceiling
[self addWallWithRect:CGRectMake(0, winSize.height, winSize.width,
1)];
```

This code is fairly self-explanatory in terms of positioning. The bottom-left corner of every Cocos2d scene is (0,0), and the CGRectMake function takes in the *x* and *y* coordinates, and then the width and height of the rectangle.

That's all for creating a simple object with some physics acting on it! Feel free to mess around with some of the variables such as elasticity, gravity, and so on.

At this point, if you notice that your objects seem to be lagging when they move across the screen—even though Xcode says the game is running at 60 FPS—add the following line of code at the top of the startScene method in AppDelegate.m:

```
[CCDirector sharedDirector].fixedUpdateInterval =
1.0f/120.f;
```

Setting gravity by tilting the device

When your user tilts the device, the device's accelerometer will pick up that information at even the slightest, most minute values. This is beneficial to those who wish to use the accelerometer (or tilting) within their game, especially with regards to moving the character or manipulating gravity, which is what we'll cover in this section.

Ever since iOS 5.0, UIAccelerometer has been replaced by the Core Motion framework data. Thankfully, it's no more complicated, so let's get started.

If you aren't a registered developer and can't use your actual device to test (and have been doing so on the simulator), note that it's not possible to test the accelerometer with the simulator unless the data can be sent to the simulator. Here's a link that might be useful in this situation: http://www.vimov.com/isimulate/.

However, even if you can't test the accelerometer on the simulator by default, it will still work as intended on anyone's device, so if you plan to include the accelerometer in your game, feel free to still follow along.

Setting up the accelerometer

Open `MainScene.h` and import the Core Motion framework:

```
#import <CoreMotion/CoreMotion.h>
```

Then add a variable for something called the `CMMotionManager`. This object will calculate the accelerometer data, and we can collect this data when we need it. Add the following line of code under the `world` variable:

```
CMMotionManager *motionManager;
```

Now open `MainScene.m`, and anywhere in the `init` method, add the following block of code so that the motion manager we just declared will begin to grab the accelerometer's data:

```
//60 times per second, in theory once per frame
CGFloat interval = 1/60.f;
motionManager = [[CMMotionManager alloc] init];
motionManager.accelerometerUpdateInterval = interval;
[motionManager startAccelerometerUpdates];
```

Right now, if you run the game, you won't notice any changes in the way it plays or any debug information. Even though the motion manager is initialized and is grabbing the data, we must set up a method to collect the data so that we can do something with it.

Reading the data

In your `init` method of `MainScene.m`, after you've initialized the motion manager, add the following line of code. It will run the specified method at the given interval (60 times per second):

```
[self schedule:@selector(getAccelerometerData:) interval:interval];
```

Then, anywhere in `MainScene.m`, we add the method we want to be called at the specified interval so that we can read the accelerometer data:

```
-(void)getAccelerometerData:(CCTime)delta
{
NSLog(@"%f\t%f\t%f",
```

```
motionManager.accelerometerData.acceleration.x, motionManager.
accelerometerData.acceleration.y, motionManager.accelerometerData.
acceleration.z);
}
```

Now, if you run the game, you'll see a lot of information being printed in the console output in Xcode. If the numbers are changing as you tilt the device, it means everything's working. Yay! If not, go back and make sure you add everything correctly.

Next, we're going to actually set the game's gravity based on how the device is rotated at any given moment.

Manipulating gravity to your heart's content

Instead of typing that long line of text every time, let's make a method with a relevant name and pass the accelerometer data. That being said, modify your `getAccelerometerData` method to the following, and add this new method, which will set the gravity of the physics world based on the accelerometer's data:

```
- (void)getAccelerometerData:(CCTime)delta
{
    //NSLog(@"%f\t%f\t%f", motionManager.accelerometerData.
acceleration.x, motionManager.accelerometerData.acceleration.y,
motionManager.accelerometerData.acceleration.z);
    [self setGravityFromAcceleration: motionManager.accelerometerData.
acceleration];
}

- (void)setGravityFromAcceleration:(CMAcceleration)accel
{
    CGFloat xGravity = 500 * accel.y;
    CGFloat yGravity = -500 * accel.x;
    world.gravity = ccp(xGravity, yGravity);
}
```

Now, if you run the game and spawn a few blocks, you'll see them floating, falling down, sliding sideways, or in whichever direction your iOS device perceives as "down." You'll probably see something similar to the following screenshot:

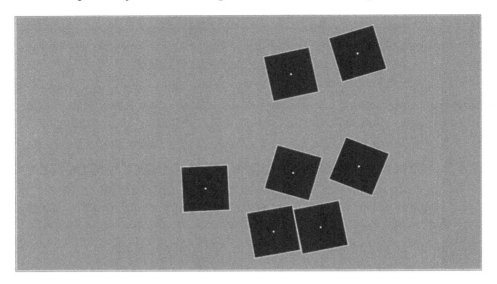

From here onwards, feel free to turn off debug draw, maybe mess around with how much gravity is set, or even change the axis the gravity is affected by.

You might notice that a square stops moving on a wall, then doesn't move when you rotate the device; that's because the object's body is sleeping. This is done to help conserve CPU processing time as well as energy when an object has no active collisions and no forces acting on it.

However, if you need them to be constantly moving, add the following line of code to your `init` method:

```
world.sleepTimeThreshold = 100000; //100,000 seconds, or about 27
hours
```

This defaults to 0.5 seconds, and why the sleeping happens when the squares stop moving against a wall. Setting it to a relatively large value, such as 100,000, will ensure that they never stop moving (that is, unless the square is sitting still for that duration, but the higher the threshold is, the less likely it is to happen).

Handling collisions in Chipmunk

It's relatively easy to handle collisions within Cocos2d when using Chipmunk (as is pretty much everything else in Cocos2d). That is why so many developers use Cocos2d. To do so, we need to do a few different steps so that Cocos2d can properly detect and handle our collisions.

Setting the collision delegate

The delegate pattern is a common way to handle messages sent by a class to any of its potential parent classes. For example, if you want to use `UITableView` (which is the standard table in `UIKit`), you must set the delegate of the table view to the class you're adding it to so that when the table view tries to refresh the data in the table, it knows which class' methods to call.

That being said, we need to tell `MainScene` that it will be a delegate for our collision handler, so open up `MainScene.h` and add `CCPhysicsCollisionDelegate` to the `@interface` line. This will allow the `CCPhysicsNode` object to set collision detection events on our `MainScene` class:

```
@interface MainScene : CCScene <CCPhysicsCollisionDelegate>
```

Then open `MainScene.m`, and in the `init` method, set the `world` object's collision delegate to `self`, like this:

```
world.collisionDelegate = self;
```

Recall that `world` is our `CCPhysicsNode` object, so any collision detection events that happen within that world (or simulation) will need to be sent somewhere to be handled further. We're setting it to `self` because self refers to the current `MainScene` instance (our currently running scene). Finally, this helps us determine which objects collide with other objects. Without this line of code, we wouldn't be able to see in the code when two objects collide, let alone tell which objects they actually are.

Although this doesn't do anything directly if you run the game now, it properly sets up your physics simulation to be able to detect and handle collisions.

Setting collision tags on game objects

Before we can create the method that will detect our collisions, we need to specify which objects will be colliding with one another. For now, we'll only be considering squares colliding with other squares.

Therefore, in the `touchBegan` method of the `MainScene.m` file, add the following line of code so that the collision detection delegate knows what object is colliding:

```
squareBody.collisionType = @"square";
```

You can do this with any physics body, but for now, this is our only object. With that in place, let's add the code to detect the actual collision between two squares.

Detecting collision

The way Chipmunk handles collisions in Cocos2d is by detecting all collisions and sending method calls to the respective functions for each collision type. So, since we're going to be detecting the collision between two squares, both parameters have to be named square. Otherwise, the method won't get called properly. The actual names of the variables of the parameters (`firstSquare` and `secondSquare`) don't matter for the sake of detection.

So, anywhere in `MainScene.m`, add the following method:

```
-(BOOL)ccPhysicsCollisionBegin:(CCPhysicsCollisionPair *)pair
square:(CCNode *)firstSquare square:(CCNode *)secondSquare
{
  NSLog(@"squares collided!");
  return YES;
}
```

If you run the game at this point, you should see the `squares collided!` text being printed to the console output every time a square collides with another. If it doesn't, go back and make sure you add everything correctly. From here onwards, you can do whatever you want when the two objects collide, as you have a pointer to both objects as well as their types.

As another example, suppose we want to detect collisions between the squares and a wall; it's very easy. First, add `wall` as `collisionType` to the body in the addWallWithRect method:

```
wallBody.collisionType = @"wall";
```

Then, add the method to detect square-wall collisions (notice the name change in the parameter from the previous `collisionBegan` method we added):

```
-(BOOL)ccPhysicsCollisionBegin:(CCPhysicsCollisionPair *)pair
square:(CCNode *)nodeA wall:(CCNode *)nodeB
{
  NSLog(@"square-wall collision!");
  return YES;
}
```

If you run the game at this point and spawn a square, as soon as it hits a wall, you should see the output being printed. And that's it for detecting collisions! Just set the `collisionDelegate` property, set the `collisionType` property, and add the collision methods.

What if you want to detect collisions on objects, but don't want them to be bouncing with other objects? In Chipmunk, you can do that.

Using Chipmunk for just collision detection

Here is an important note: if you're going to just detect one of the following, you do not need to use a physics engine for your collision detection, but rather the listed method:

- For rectangles intersecting rectangles, use `CGRectIntersectsRect`
- For points inside rectangles, use `CGRectContainsPoint`
- For radius/distance intersection, use `ccpDistance`

If you're going to be detecting collisions with non-rectangular and noncircular objects, feel free to read on.

Sometimes, all you're doing is sending objects across the screen, or rotating them with your custom actions, and you just want to know when two objects collide, but don't want the bouncing, pushing, and colliding that comes with the entire physics engine. Luckily, we can do that in Chipmunk.

Turning the physics body into a sensor

Sensors, with respect to Chipmunk, are basically bodies that can detect collisions, but pass right through other bodies. These are helpful when you have areas or sections of the screen that trigger certain events, but don't actually cause any physics-based interactions.

For example, if you're making a top-down mini golf game with a physics engine and you want to include ramps, the best way to do this is to set the ramp as a sensor. When the ball and ramp collide, set the gravity in a certain direction.

To make a body a sensor, simply set the `sensor` variable to true, like this:

```
[squareBody setSensor:YES];
```

If you run the game now, you'll notice that the blocks fall right through one another, as well as right through the floor.

And that's it! All you need is the collision handling (in the previous section), and the sensor variable set to true. Any physics body that's a sensor will trigger collision detection events, but not cause any movement or changes to other bodies.

Summary

Throughout this chapter, you learned how to create a physics simulation, add bodies to the simulation, set the gravity of the world with the accelerometer, handle collisions, and even use the simulation for just collision detection.

When it comes to really complex physics engine mechanics, such as ropes, joints, and pivots, the Cocos2d documentation at `http://www.cocos2d-swift.org/docs/api/index.html` explains a lot. At the time of writing this book, there are very few (if any) tutorials on such complex mechanics available.

In the next chapter, you'll learn about sound in Cocos2d and some of the cool things you can do to sound effects within the engine.

4

Sound and Music

This chapter is all about the different ways to present music and sound effects to the player of the game using Cocos2d, and why high-quality music and sound effects matter in a great game. Trust me, there's more to sound effects than just playing a sound file when an event happens. Otherwise, why would it have an entire chapter? Although there are a lot of users who play with the sound off on mobile devices, it's still an immersive part of some players' experience, so we have to pay close attention to not only the sounds we choose but also how they're implemented.

In this chapter, we will cover the following topics:

- Loading and unloading effects
- Playing sound effects and loop background music in creative ways
- Modifying the played sound on the fly
- Other good examples of sounds

For the code up to this point, open the **Chapter 4** project and the sound effects from the Sounds directory in the book's included files.

It's recommended that you follow the code provided, as this chapter, along with future chapters, will be referencing methods and classes that are provided or mentioned within the book.

If there are any gameplay bugs or imbalances in the prototype, that's fine; we'll cover polishing in a later chapter. Remember, the prototype was done quickly with the sole purpose of showing others the core concept of the game, not providing them with a finished product.

Prerequisites

Make sure you've copied the sound files to your project. If they aren't there, no matter how many times you try to preload, unload, play, or loop, the sound files simply won't play. Unlike the sprite sheets used with TexturePacker and the BMFonts created with Glyph Designer, it's best to drag the sound files into your project and have the **Copy items if needed** checkbox checked, as shown in the following screenshot. This will ensure that the files are in your project until you decide to delete them.

Seeing the difference in audio types

If you're wondering what the differences are between MP3, CAF, and other file and data formats for audio, check out `http://www.raywenderlich.com/69365/audio-tutorial-ios-file-data-formats-2014-edition`, a detailed explanation on all the different types of audio. It's not necessary for this book, but if you're trying to save space or wondering if you can use certain audio files, this link will be helpful.

We're going to be using MP3 in this chapter (and subsequently in the rest of the book's content) as it's a very common format, as well as a format that's supported by OALSimpleAudio and the iPhone natively.

Learning about OALSimpleAudio

If you've ever wanted an easy way to play sound files, OALSimpleAudio is the thing you need. It can very easily load a large variety of sound files, play effects, loop background music, and a lot more. Its existence and integration with Cocos2d makes it much easier to bring your game to life with the immersive capabilities of sound and music.

 If you've programmed in Cocos2d before and are wondering where SimpleAudioEngine is, starting in Cocos2d v3.0, OALSimpleAudio is the new way to play sound effects. It's basically everything that SimpleAudioEngine was.

Preloading effects

If you try to play an effect using OALSimpleAudio, there will be a slight freeze, or delay, as the device tries to quickly load the effect into the memory and then play it right away. Luckily, there's a way to load the sound effects and music such that it doesn't freeze in front of your users when you try to play an effect.

OALSimpleAudio allows preloading of effects, which essentially reads the sound effect into the memory long before you'll need the effect. The choice is up to you whether to do this at the beginning of the game (when users first launch it from their home screen), or between levels by unloading and reloading the effects for the upcoming level. The way to load sound files into the memory with OALSimpleAudio is by adding the following line of code:

```
ALBuffer *buffer = [[OALSimpleAudio sharedInstance]
preloadEffect:@"soundEffect.mp3"];
```

The `buffer` variable assignment is optional and is used if you need to print out various pieces of information about the sound file such as frequency or bits of the buffer.

 Although the preceding code example shows `.mp3` as the file extension, OALSimpleAudio can load any sound file that's supported by iOS.

However, if you want to cut down on the time it takes to load all your in-game sounds, you can do so in the background, which is known as loading asynchronously.

Loading files asynchronously

Loading your files asynchronously is the best way to cut down on load time while simultaneously getting all the files loaded. However, note that because loading this way occurs in the background, there's no guarantee that the files will be ready when the user begins to interact with your game.

If you wish to make certain sound effects available for them at the beginning of the game (at the loading screen, before the main menu starts, right when the main menu starts, or whatever you see the beginning of your game as), it's recommended to load the minimum amount of sound needed if you still wish to load the majority of your effects asynchronously.

The way to do this is with the following line of code. It will push the loading into the background and notify you when it's done:

```
__block ALBuffer *soundBuffer;
[[OALSimpleAudio sharedInstance] preloadEffect:@"soundEffect.mp3"
reduceToMono:NO completionBlock:^(ALBuffer* buffer)
{
  soundBuffer = buffer;
}];
```

Unloading effects

If you know you're not going to use the sound effect for a while, or you often run into memory warnings, unloading your sound effects can be useful. For example, if your game uses a certain sound file for a voice-over in the tutorial only, once the user passes the tutorial, you can unload this sound effect to free up some memory. OALSimpleAudio will not unload sound effects that are either playing or paused.

To unload a specific sound effect, you can use this line of code:

```
[[OALSimpleAudio sharedInstance] unloadEffect:@"soundEffect.mp3"];
```

To unload all your sound effects at once, you can use the following line of code:

```
[[OALSimpleAudio sharedInstance] unloadAllEffects];
```

 A recommended place to put these unloading calls is your `applicationDidReceiveMemoryWarning` method in the `AppDelegate` class.

Playing sound effects and loop background music

Obviously, you wouldn't just want to be loading and unloading your sound effects all day, so let's get into the actual playing of these sounds here.

Getting some background music going

It's always important to set the tone of the voice through the music that gets played in the background. Whether that means a bleak, withering tone or a happy-go-lucky, upbeat tone, the music can help bring in the player so that they become more engaged with the game.

Because the background music will likely be playing for the majority of the time throughout the game, it's not entirely important to preload it. However, it's still recommended, as it will prevent the slight bit of lag at the beginning of the game when the music first starts playing. You can preload the background music using the following code:

```
[[OALSimpleAudio sharedInstance]
preloadBg:@"backgroundMusic.mp3"];
```

With the preceding line of code added, you can simply play the background music on loop with one call. To play preloaded background music, add this line of code:

```
[[OALSimpleAudio sharedInstance] playBgWithLoop:YES];
```

So, for this book's project, we're going to play background music throughout the time the game is being played. Thus, we want the user to be immersed as early as possible, so we're going to preload the background music even before the first scene loads, and start playing it as soon as possible. Open AppDelegate.m, and go to the startScene method. Right above the return statement, add this line of code:

```
[[OALSimpleAudio sharedInstance]
preloadBg:@"backgroundMusic.mp3"];
```

Now that we have made OALSimpleAudio aware of what our background music is, we can immediately play the file on loop, so by the time the first scene gets displayed, there's already music playing. So, right below the preloading line, add this:

```
[[OALSimpleAudio sharedInstance] playBgWithLoop:YES];
```

Isn't that lovely? But background music alone isn't going to be enough. Let's add in some sound effects when the user does different activities in the game.

Sounds when a button is clicked on

One of the human psychological traits that exists is the desire for feedback when an action is taken. Thus, when a button is pressed in digital space, we need to give the user feedback that their action has been received. This is why the button darkens slightly to indicate that it's being pressed down. Upon release of this button, we'd like to also play a sound effect telling the user their action is being processed.

To play a sound effect when a button is pressed in Cocos2d, just add the line of code required to play the sound file to whichever method the button calls. So, for this project, open `MainScene.m`, go to the `goToMenu` method, and add this line of code right before the line where the `replaceScene` method gets called:

```
[[OALSimpleAudio sharedInstance] playEffect:@"buttonClick.mp3"];
```

This will play the sound effect once, right before everything starts to load for the next scene. Do the same for the **Restart** button, by going to the `restartGame` method and the `goToGame` method in `MenuScene.m`:

```
- (void) restartGame
{
    [[OALSimpleAudio sharedInstance] playEffect:@"buttonClick.mp3"];
    [[CCDirector sharedDirector] replaceScene:[MainScene scene]];
}

- (void) goToGame
{
    [[OALSimpleAudio sharedInstance] playEffect:@"buttonClick.mp3"];
    [[CCDirector sharedDirector] replaceScene:[MainScene scene]];
}
```

 If you notice a slight delay before the sound effect the first time you click on a button, that's a sign that you should preload the sound effect before the user can press the given button.

Now, if all we have is background music and button clicks, we surely need to engross the user even more. Thus, we'll add some sound when the user moves a unit distance on the game board.

Sounds on unit movements

Similar to the button click effects, we want to play the effect whenever the `moveUnit` method gets called. Why here and not in the `Unit` class? Because, if we called it in the Unit class, we'd possibly be calling the method 81 times at once (9 x 9 grid). Yes, this is hard to obtain, but technically possible. Calling it up to 81 times at once will cause the effects to stack on top of each other and become a lot louder than we want.

So, open `MainScene.m` and go to the `moveUnit` method. Here, right after we update the position of the unit the user wants to move, we'll play the sound effect:

```
-(void)moveUnit:(NSNotification*)notif
{
  NSDictionary *userInfo = [notif userInfo];
  Unit *u = (Unit*)userInfo[@"unit"];
  u.position = [self getPositionForGridCoord:u.gridPos];

// Add this line:
  [[OALSimpleAudio sharedInstance] playEffect:@"moveUnit.mp3"];

  ++numTurnSurvived;

  // ..etc..
}
```

When you run the game and move a unit, you should hear a very subtle sound. The reason it's so subtle is that the user will be doing this for the entire game. We don't want to overwhelm them with the movement sound effect, as it might irritate some players, causing them to turn the sound off or simply quit playing, the latter of which we don't want to happen.

Sounds on unit combination

Although the movement happens literally every turn (or else a turn won't happen), two units combining may not be the case every turn. Therefore, we want to give the player a rewarding feeling when they combine two weak units to make one strong unit.

Because our unit combination code is a bit scattered, we have to be careful where to place the code so that the unit combination sound effect happens only once per combination. For example, if all three units move into one square at the same time, we should only play the effect only once instead of twice by accident. This makes it a bit tricky, but for now, let's not worry about the three- or four-unit combinations, and just handle the two-unit combinations. It's going to play twice and three times respectively for the three- and four-unit combinations, but that's okay for an early version of the game.

First, open your `MainScene.m` file and add this method anywhere in your code:

```
-(void)playUnitCombineSoundWithValue:(NSInteger)total
{
}
```

Then go to the `checkForAnyDirectionCombineWithUnit` method and add the following lines of code right under the `NSInteger fv` and `NSInteger ov` lines (`fv` and `ov` stand for first value and other value respectively, and they will hold the values of the first unit and the other unit that get passed to this method):

```
if (first.isFriendly)
[self playUnitCombineSoundWithValue:fv+ov];
```

Also, go to the `checkForCombineWithUnit` method and add these lines of code at the same spot (below the two `NSInteger` declarations).

The reason we have the `if` statement is that we need to make sure the sound effect only plays when a friendly unit is combined with another friendly unit. We don't need to check `other` because we only call this method with two units of the same type. As for the `fv+ov` and `total` parameters, those will be used later in this chapter, so just hold on for now.

Lastly, in the `playUnitCombineSound` method, you'll need to add the following line of code so that the effect actually plays:

```
[[OALSimpleAudio sharedInstance] playEffect:@"unitCombine.mp3"];
```

If you run the game now, you will hear a sound when one friendly unit combines with another. There's just one more type of sound effect we want to add in this early version of the game.

Sounds when the user loses

Last but not least, we want to include some sounds that play when a user loses their game. It's not entirely motivating to hear the losing sound effect over and over, but it is effective in keep user retention high, as it emphasizes the "let me try that one more time, I almost had it" feeling. Picking the right sound for this can be a bit hard, but once you've found a sound effect that you feel is sufficient, you can go ahead and add it to the **Game Over** screen.

So first, we need a **Game Over** screen to exist. Similar to the Unit class, create a GameOverScene class with a subclass of type CCScene. Your GameOverScene.h file should look something like this:

```
#import "CCScene.h"

@interface GameOverScene : CCScene
{
  CGSize winSize;
}

@property (nonatomic, assign) NSInteger numUnitsKilled;
@property (nonatomic, assign) NSInteger numTotalScore;
@property (nonatomic, assign) NSInteger numTurnsSurvived;

+(CCScene*)scene;
@end
```

Then open your GameOverScene.m file. It looks something like this:

```
#import "GameOverScene.h"

@implementation GameOverScene

+(CCScene*)scene
{
  return [[self alloc] init];
}

-(id)init
{
```

```
    if ((self=[super init]))
    {
       winSize = [[CCDirector sharedDirector] viewSize];

       //these values range 0 to 1.0, so use float to get ratio
       CCNode *background = [CCNodeColor nodeWithColor:[CCColor
colorWithRed:128/255.f green:0/255.f blue:88/255.f]];
       [self addChild:background];


    }
    return self;
}

- (void)goToMenu
{
    //to be filled in later
}

- (void)restartGame
{
    //to be filled in later
}
@end
```

In the `init` method of the `GameOverScene`, we want the Game Over sound effect to play. We're adding it here so that the sound effect plays as soon as the Game Over scene loads. So, right under the line of code for the background color, add the following to play the Game Over sound effect:

```
[[OALSimpleAudio sharedInstance] playEffect:@"gameOver.mp3"];
```

To hear the sound play, we need to send the user to the GameOverScene when they lose, so go to the `endGame` method in the `MainScene.m` file, and change that line of code to this (don't forget to add the `#include "GameOverScene.h"` line of code at the top of the file):

```
[[CCDirector sharedDirector] replaceScene:[GameOverScene scene]];
```

And there you have it—a Game Over sound effect! So, up to this point, we have all the sound effects in place: the unit movements, the combinations, Game Over, the background music, and so on. But after a while, the sound gets a little repetitive, so let's modify the sounds a bit to lessen the annoyance of a repeated sound.

Modifying the sound effect on the fly

One thing that's so cool about using OALSimpleAudio (and was also true about SimpleAudioEngine) is that you can modify how the audio file sounds when it gets played back to the user. For example, if you wish to have a series of coins collected, and each coin collected in rapid succession plays a slightly higher-pitched sound than the previous one, you can simply modify the pitch based on how many coins were collected.

The volume (or gain), pitch, and pan

With one simple call that adds a few parameters to the default `playEffect` method, you can modify the loudness of the effect, the pitch of the sound effect, and where in the speakers your effect plays. You can do so with the following code:

```
//volume range: 0.0 to 1.0
//pitch range: 0.0 to inf (1.0 is normal)
//pan range:  -1.0 to 1.0 (far left to far right)
//loop:  If YES, will play until stop is called on the sound
[[OALSimpleAudio sharedInstance] playEffect:@"soundEffect.mp3"
volume:1 pitch:1 pan:1 loop:NO];
```

Stopping looped sound effects

If you've said "Yes" to the preceding loop and wish to stop it at some point, you have to grab the return value of the preceding function, like this:

```
id<ALSoundSource> effect;

effect = [[OALSimpleAudio sharedInstance]
playEffect:@"soundEffect.mp3" volume:1 pitch:1 pan:1 loop:NO];
```

Then call the respective stop function on the variable:

```
[effect stop];
```

Modifying the combine sound effect

Ideally, we don't want the user to hear the same sound effect over and over every time they combine units. Not only will it become obnoxious and annoying to the user but it will also make the game feel more boring and less exciting. With that said, we want to modify the combining sound effect so slightly so that as the user gets a higher number of unit combinations, they feel emboldened by their success, making them wish to play longer.

One of the approaches is to modify the pitch of the sound effect. This will work up to a certain point, until the sound effect becomes so pushed in one direction that it's simply better to provide another sound effect for truly large unit combinations.

Open the `MainScene.m` file and scroll to the `playUnitCombineSoundWithValue` method. Here, you're going to modify the code to look something like this:

```
CGFloat pitchValue = 1.0 - (total / 100.f);
//eg: fv+ov = 20 ... 1.0 - 0.2 = 0.8
if (total < 50)
{
  [[OALSimpleAudio sharedInstance] playEffect:@"unitCombine.mp3"
    volume:1 pitch:pitchValue pan:0 loop:NO];
}

else
{
  [[OALSimpleAudio sharedInstance]
    playEffect:@"largeUnitCombine.mp3"];
}
```

When you run the game and combine a unit, you will hear the sound effect getting deeper and deeper until a certain value (the tipping point—in this case, a new unit value of 50 or more). At this point, we want to play a different sound effect, which is what the inner `if` statement handles.

Other great sound places

The following are a couple of examples of games that make great use of sound effects. These games not only engage the user more, but are also great examples of how you can use sound effects for more than just basic events such as simple user movements or button clicks:

- *Threes!*: This game has faces on the cards, and if you don't do anything, after a few moments, you'll hear the cards making random noises. Also, if you try to slide the cards into a position that doesn't move anything (an invalid move), you will hear one of the cards say "Nope!" It's really cute and is just another way the ambience of the game is upheld through the sounds. Take a look at the UI of the game, as shown in the following screenshot:

- *Crossy Road*: In this game, every now and then, you'll come across a vehicle that's playing music, a police car, or a garbage truck. All of these are fairly rare, but when the player experiences them and hears the extra level of sound, it becomes more enjoyable, as it's not just another car driving by. Plus, with all the cars and trains in the game, if you're wearing headphones, you'll hear the vehicle's music go from one ear to the other. Have a look at the UI of this game:

Summary

This chapter taught you how to preload, unload, play, and modify sound files using OALSimpleAudio and Cocos2d. You also saw some cool ways in which we integrated the use of sound in this book's project. Because the game is still in that prototype-esque phase, the sounds may change or be modified. However, the vast majority of them are implemented. Also, if you want to learn how to turn on/off sound or music in your game via an option in the menu or settings, read *Chapter 6, Tidying Up and Polishing*, as that chapter will cover more such details.

There are also a lot of situational methods in OALSimpleAudio that were not covered in this chapter. If you wish to read more about them, you can view the documentation at http://www.learn-cocos2d.com/api-ref/1.0/ObjectAL/html/interface_o_a_l_simple_audio.html#aaf877e4f0526408d569fd12f37e8e1f7.

In the next chapter, we'll cover some really cool concepts and mechanics that most game developers don't take time to implement in their game — and it's more than just Game Center or iCloud support.

5

Creating Cool Content

In this chapter, you'll be learning how to implement the really complex, subtle game mechanics that not many developers do. This is what separates the good games from the great games. There will be many examples, tutorials, and code snippets in this chapter intended for adaption in your own projects, so feel free to come back at any time to look at something you may have either missed the first time, or are just curious to know about in general.

In this chapter, we will cover the following topics:

- Adding a table for scores
- Adding subtle sliding to the units
- Creating movements on a Bézier curve instead of straight paths
- Depth perception via device tilting (and parallax scrolling)
- Three ways to create unit streamers or ghosts
- Touchscreen controls versus D-pad adaptation (and why it matters so much to know this distinction)
- A common theme for this chapter will be to show you how to take what seem like complex things and turn them into easy-to-code and easy-to-modify segments that you can implement in your own project (or projects).

Also, this chapter features things that won't go well with the book's project, and only the first two points in the preceding list are related to the game project, which has been slowly worked all this while. The rest are standalone sample projects with code designed in a modular fashion so that you can extract it for your own projects faster.

It's strongly recommended to open the Chapter 5 code before working on the first two sections. A decent amount of code has been added and/or modified since the last chapter, and it was not talked about in this book. Therefore, you may get compilation errors should you try to follow along with the book without using the Chapter 5 project code. Thanks for understanding!

Adding a table for scores

Because we want a way to show the user their past high scores, in the GameOver scene, we're going to add a table that displays the most recent high scores that are saved. For this, we're going to use CCTableView. It's still relatively new, but it works for what we're going to use it.

CCTableView versus UITableView

Although UITableView might be known to some of you who've made non-Cocos2d apps before, you should be aware of its downfalls when it comes to using it within Cocos2d. For example, if you want a BMFont in your table, you can't add LabelBMFont (you could try to convert the BMFont into a TTF font and use that within the table, but that's outside the scope of this book).

If you still wish to use a UITableView object (or any UIKit element for that matter), you can create the object like normal, and add it to the scene, like this (tblScores is the name of the UITableView object):

```
[[[CCDirector sharedDirector] view] addSubview:tblScores];
```

Saving high scores (NSUserDefaults)

Before we display any high scores, we have to make sure we save them. The easiest way to do this is by making use of Apple's built-in data preservation tool—NSUserDefaults. If you've never used it before, let me tell you that it's basically a dictionary with "save" mechanics that stores the values in the device so that the next time the user loads the device, the values are available for the app.

Also, because there are three different values we're tracking for each gameplay, let's only say a given game is better than another game when the total score is greater.

Therefore, let's create a `saveHighScore` method that will go through all the total scores in our saved list and see whether the current total score is greater than any of the saved scores. If so, it will insert itself and bump the rest down. In `MainScene.m`, add the following method:

```
-(NSInteger)saveHighScore
{
  //save top 20 scores

  //an array of Dictionaries...
  //keys in each dictionary:
  //   [DictTotalScore]
  //   [DictTurnsSurvived]
  //   [DictUnitsKilled]

//read the array of high scores saved on the user's device
  NSMutableArray *arrScores = [[[NSUserDefaults standardUserDefaults]
arrayForKey:DataHighScores] mutableCopy];

//sentinel value of -1 (in other words, if a high score was not found
on this play through)
  NSInteger index = -1;
//loop through the scores in the array
  for (NSDictionary *dictHighScore in arrScores)
    {
//if the current game's total score is greater than the score stored
in the current index of the array...
    if (numTotalScore > [dictHighScore[DictTotalScore] integerValue])
      {
//then store that index and break out of the loop
      index = [arrScores indexOfObject:dictHighScore];
      break;
      }
    }

//if a new high score was found
  if (index > -1)
    {
//create a dictionary to store the score, turns survived, and units
killed
```

```
        NSDictionary *newHighScore = @{ DictTotalScore : @(numTotalScore),
        DictTurnsSurvived : @(numTurnSurvived),
        DictUnitsKilled : @(numUnitsKilled) };

    //then insert that dictionary into the array of high scores
        [arrScores insertObject:newHighScore atIndex:index];

    //remove the very last object in the high score list (in other words,
    limit the number of scores)
        [arrScores removeLastObject];

    //then save the array
        [[NSUserDefaults standardUserDefaults] setObject:arrScores
    forKey:DataHighScores];
        [[NSUserDefaults standardUserDefaults] synchronize];
    }

    //finally return the index of the high score (whether it's -1 or an
    actual value within the array)
        return index;
    }
```

Finally, call this method in the endGame method right before you transition to the next scene:

```
- (void) endGame
{
    //call the method here to save the high score, then grab the index
    of the high score within the array
    NSInteger hsIndex = [self saveHighScore];

    NSDictionary *scoreData = @{ DictTotalScore : @(numTotalScore),
    DictTurnsSurvived : @(numTurnSurvived),
    DictUnitsKilled : @(numUnitsKilled),
    DictHighScoreIndex : @(hsIndex)};

    [[CCDirector sharedDirector] replaceScene:[GameOverScene
    sceneWithScoreData:scoreData]];

}
```

Now that we have our high scores being saved, let's create the table to display them.

Creating the table

It's really simple to set up a CCTableView object. All we need to do is modify the contentSize object, and then put in a few methods that handle the size and content of each cell.

So first, open the GameOverScene.h file and set the scene as a data source for the CCTableView:

```
@interface GameOverScene : CCScene <CCTableViewDataSource>
```

Then, in the initWithScoreData method, create the header labels as well as initialize the CCTableView:

```
//get the high score array from the user's device
arrScores = [[NSUserDefaults standardUserDefaults]
arrayForKey:DataHighScores];

//create labels
CCLabelBMFont *lblTableTotalScore = [CCLabelBMFont
labelWithString:@"Total Score:" fntFile:@"bmFont.fnt"];

CCLabelBMFont *lblTableUnitsKilled = [CCLabelBMFont
labelWithString:@"Units Killed:" fntFile:@"bmFont.fnt"];

CCLabelBMFont *lblTableTurnsSurvived = [CCLabelBMFont
labelWithString:@"Turns Survived:" fntFile:@"bmFont.fnt"];

//position the labels
lblTableTotalScore.position = ccp(winSize.width * 0.5, winSize.height
* 0.85);
lblTableUnitsKilled.position = ccp(winSize.width * 0.675, winSize.
height * 0.85);
lblTableTurnsSurvived.position = ccp(winSize.width * 0.875, winSize.
height * 0.85);

//add the labels to the scene
[self addChild:lblTableTurnsSurvived];
[self addChild:lblTableTotalScore];
[self addChild:lblTableUnitsKilled];

//create the tableview and add it to the scene
CCTableView * tblScores = [CCTableView node];
tblScores.contentSize = CGSizeMake(0.6, 0.4);
```

```
CGFloat ratioX = (1.0 - tblScores.contentSize.width) * 0.75;
CGFloat ratioY = (1.0 - tblScores.contentSize.height) / 2;
tblScores.position = ccp(winSize.width * ratioX, winSize.height *
ratioY);
tblScores.dataSource = self;
tblScores.block = ^(CCTableView *table){
    //if the press a cell, do something here.
    //NSLog(@"Cell %ld", (long)table.selectedRow);
};
[self addChild: tblScores];
```

With the `CCTableView` object's data source being set to `self` we can add the three methods that will determine exactly how our table looks and what data goes in each cell (that is, row).

 Note that if we don't set the data source, the table view's method will not be called; and if we set it to anything other than `self`, the methods will be called on that object/class instead.

That being said, add these three methods:

```
-(CCTableViewCell*)tableView:(CCTableView *)tableView
nodeForRowAtIndex:(NSUInteger)index
{
   CCTableViewCell* cell = [CCTableViewCell node];

   cell.contentSizeType = CCSizeTypeMake(CCSizeUnitNormalized,
CCSizeUnitPoints);
   cell.contentSize = CGSizeMake(1, 40);

   // Color every other row differently
   CCNodeColor* bg;
   if (index % 2 != 0) bg = [CCNodeColor nodeWithColor:[CCColor
colorWithRed:0 green:0 blue:0 alpha:0.3]];
   else bg = [CCNodeColor nodeWithColor: [CCColor colorWithRed:0
green:0 blue:0 alpha:0.2]];

   bg.userInteractionEnabled = NO;
   bg.contentSizeType = CCSizeTypeNormalized;
   bg.contentSize = CGSizeMake(1, 1);
   [cell addChild:bg];
   return cell;
}
```

```
- (NSUInteger)tableViewNumberOfRows:(CCTableView *)tableView
{
    return [arrScores count];
}

- (float)tableView:(CCTableView *)tableView
heightForRowAtIndex:(NSUInteger)index
{
    return 40.f;
}
```

The first method, `tableView:nodeForRowAtIndex:`, will format each cell based on which index it is. For now, we're going to color each cell in one of two different colors.

The second method, `tableViewNumberOfRows:`, returns the number of rows, or cells, that will be in the table view. Since we know there are going to be 20, we can technically type 20, but what if we decide to change that number later? So, let's stick with using the count of the array.

The third method, `tableView:heightForRowAtIndex:`, is meant to return the height of the row, or cell, at the given index. Since we aren't doing anything different with any cell in particular, we can hardcode this value to a fairly reasonable height of 40.

At this point, you should be able to run the game, and when you lose, you'll be taken to the game over screen with the labels across the top as well as a table that scrolls on the right side of the screen.

It's good practice when learning Cocos2d to just mess around with stuff to see what sort of effects you can make. For example, you could try using some ScaleTo actions to scale the text up from 0, or use a MoveTo action to slide it from the bottom or the side.

Feel free to see whether you can create a cool way to display the text right now.

Now that we have the table in place, let's get the data displayed, shall we?

Showing the scores

Now that we have our table created, it's a simple addition to our code to get the proper numbers to display correctly.

In the `nodeForRowAtIndex` method, add the following block of code right after adding the background color to the cell:

```
//Create the 4 labels that will be used within the cell (row).
CCLabelBMFont *lblScoreNumber = [CCLabelBMFont
labelWithString:[NSString stringWithFormat:@"%d)", index+1]
fntFile:@"bmFont.fnt"];
//Set the anchor point to the middle-right (default middle-middle)
lblScoreNumber.anchorPoint = ccp(1,0.5);

CCLabelBMFont *lblTotalScore = [CCLabelBMFont
labelWithString:[NSString stringWithFormat:@"%d", [arrScores[index]
[DictTotalScore] integerValue]] fntFile:@"bmFont.fnt"];

CCLabelBMFont *lblUnitsKilled = [CCLabelBMFont
labelWithString:[NSString stringWithFormat:@"%d", [arrScores[index]
[DictUnitsKilled] integerValue]] fntFile:@"bmFont.fnt"];

CCLabelBMFont *lblTurnsSurvived = [CCLabelBMFont
labelWithString:[NSString stringWithFormat:@"%d", [arrScores[index]
[DictTurnsSurvived] integerValue]] fntFile:@"bmFont.fnt"];

//set the position type of each label to normalized (where (0,0)
is the bottom left of its parent and (1,1) is the top right of its
parent)
lblScoreNumber.positionType = lblTotalScore.positionType =
lblUnitsKilled.positionType = lblTurnsSurvived.positionType =
CCPositionTypeNormalized;

//position all of the labels within the cell
lblScoreNumber.position = ccp(0.15,0.5);
lblTotalScore.position = ccp(0.35,0.5);
lblUnitsKilled.position = ccp(0.6,0.5);
lblTurnsSurvived.position = ccp(0.9,0.5);

//if the index we're iterating through is the same index as our High
Score index...
if (index == highScoreIndex)
{
//then set the color of all the labels to a golden color
    lblScoreNumber.color =
    lblTotalScore.color =
```

```
    lblUnitsKilled.color =
    lblTurnsSurvived.color = [CCColor colorWithRed:1 green:183/255.f
blue:0];
}


//add all of the labels to the individual cell
[cell addChild:lblScoreNumber];
[cell addChild:lblTurnsSurvived];
[cell addChild:lblTotalScore];
[cell addChild:lblUnitsKilled];
```

And that's it! When you play the game and end up at the game over screen, you'll see the high scores being displayed (even the scores from earlier attempts, because they were saved, remember?). Notice the high score that is yellow. It's an indication that the score you got in the game you just played is on the scoreboard, and shows you where it is.

Although the CCTableView might feel a bit weird with things disappearing and reappearing as you scroll, we'll cover how to make that better in the next chapter on polishing our game. For now, let's get some *Threes!* — like sliding into our game.

If you're considering adding a CCTableView to your own project, the key takeaway here is to make sure you modify the contentSize and position properly. By default, the contentSize is a normalized CGSize, so from 0 to 1, and the anchor point is (0,0).

Plus, make sure you perform these two steps:

- Set the data source of the table view
- Add the three table view methods

With all that in mind, it should be relatively easy to implement a CCTableView.

Adding subtle sliding to the units

If you've ever played *Threes!* (or if you haven't, check out the trailer at http://asherv.com/threes/, and maybe even download the game on your phone), you would be aware of the sliding feature when a user begins to make their move but hasn't yet completed the move. At the speed of the dragging finger, the units slide in the direction they're going to move, showing the user where each unit will go and how each unit will combine with another.

This is useful as it not only adds that extra layer of "cool factor" but also provides a preview of the future for the user if they want to revert their decision ahead of time and make a different, more calculated move.

Here's a side note: if you want your game to go really viral, you have to make the user believe it was their fault that they lost, and not your "stupid game mechanics" (as some players might say).

Think *Angry Birds, Smash Hit, Crossy Road, Threes!, Tiny Wings…* the list goes on and on with more games that became popular, and all had one underlying theme: when the user loses, it was entirely in their control to win or lose, and they made the wrong move.

This unseen mechanic pushes players to play again with a better strategy in mind. And this is exactly why we want our users to see their move before it gets made. It's a win-win situation for both the developers and the players.

Sliding one unit

If we can get one unit to slide, we can surely get the rest of the units to slide by simply looping through them, modularizing the code, or some other form of generalization.

That being said, we need to set up the `Unit` class so that it can detect how far the finger has dragged. Thus, we can determine how far to move the unit. So, open `Unit.h` and add the following variable. It will track the distance from the previous touch position:

```
@property (nonatomic, assign) CGPoint previousTouchPos;
```

Then, in the `touchMoved` method of `Unit.m`, add the following assignment to `previousTouchPos`. It sets the previous touch position to the touch-down position, but only after the distance is greater than 20 units:

```
if (!self.isBeingDragged && ccpDistance(touchPos, self.touchDownPos) >
20)
{
  self.isBeingDragged = YES;
  //add it here:
  self.previousTouchPos = self.touchDownPos;
```

Once that's in place, we can begin calculating the distance while the finger is being dragged. To do that, we'll do a simple check. Add the following block of code at the end of `touchMoved`, after the end of the initial `if` block:

```
//only if the unit is currently being dragged
if (self.isBeingDragged)
{
    CGFloat dist = 0;
    //if the direction the unit is being dragged is either UP or
      DOWN
    if (self.dragDirection == DirUp || self.dragDirection == DirDown)
    //then subtract the current touch position's Y-value from the
      previously-recorded Y-value to determine the distance to
      move
      dist = touchPos.y - self.previousTouchPos.y;
      //else if the direction the unit is being dragged is either
        LEFT or RIGHT
    else if (self.dragDirection == DirLeft ||
        self.dragDirection == DirRight)
        //then subtract the current touch position's Y-value from
          the previously-recorded Y-value to determine the
          distance to move
      dist = touchPos.x - self.previousTouchPos.x;

    //then assign the touch position for the next iteration of touchMoved
    to work properly
    self.previousTouchPos = touchPos;

}
```

The assignment of `previousTouchPos` at the end will ensure that while the unit is being dragged, we continue to update the touch position so that we can determine the distance. Plus, the distance is calculated in only the direction in which the unit is being dragged (up and down are denoted by Y, and left and right are denoted by X).

Now that we have the distance between finger drags being calculated, let's push this into a function that will move our unit based on which direction it's being dragged in. So, right after you've calculated `dist` in the previous code block, call the following method to move our unit based on the amount dragged:

```
dist /= 2; //optional
[self slideUnitWithDistance:dist
withDragDirection:self.dragDirection];
```

Dividing the distance by 2 is optional. You may think the squares are too small, and want the user to be able to see their square. So note that dividing by 2, or a larger number, will mean that for every 1 point the finger moves, the unit will move by 1/2 (or less) points.

With that method call being ready, we need to implement it, so add the following method body for now. Since this method is rather complicated, it's going to be added in parts:

```
-(void)slideUnitWithDistance:(CGFloat)dist withDragDirection:(enum
UnitDirection)dir
{
}
```

The first thing we need to do is set up a variable to calculate the new x and y positions of the unit. We'll call these newX and newY, and set them to the unit's current position:

```
CGFloat newX = self.position.x, newY = self.position.y;
```

Next, we want to grab the position that the unit starts at, that is, the position the unit would be at if it was positioned at its current grid coordinate. To do that, we're going to call the getPositionForGridCoordinate method from MainScene, (since that's where the positions are being calculated anyway, we might as well use that function):

```
CGPoint originalPos = [MainScene
getPositionForGridCoord:self.gridPos];
```

Next, we're going to move the newX or newY based on the direction in which the unit is being dragged. For now, let's just add the up direction:

```
if (self.dragDirection == DirUp)
{
    newY += dist;
    if (newY > originalPos.y + self.gridWidth)
      newY = originalPos.y + self.gridWidth;
    else if (newY < originalPos.y)
      newY = originalPos.y;
}
```

In this if block, we're first going to add the distance to the `newY` variable (because we're going up, we're adding to Y instead of X). Then, we want to make sure the position is at most 1 square up. We're going to use the `gridWidth` (which is essentially the width of the square, assigned in the `initCommon` method). Also, we need to make sure that if they're bringing the square back to its original position, it doesn't go into the square beneath it.

So let's add the rest of the directions as else if statements:

```
else if (self.dragDirection == DirDown)
{
    newY += dist;
    if (newY < originalPos.y - self.gridWidth)
      newY = originalPos.y - self.gridWidth;
    else if (newY > originalPos.y)
      newY = originalPos.y;
}
else if (self.dragDirection == DirLeft)
{
    newX += dist;
    if (newX < originalPos.x - self.gridWidth)
      newX = originalPos.x - self.gridWidth;
    else if (newX > originalPos.x)
      newX = originalPos.x;
}
else if (self.dragDirection == DirRight)
{
    newX += dist;
    if (newX > originalPos.x + self.gridWidth)
      newX = originalPos.x + self.gridWidth;
    else if (newX < originalPos.x)
      newX = originalPos.x;
}
```

Finally, we will set the position of the unit based on the newly calculated *x* and *y* positions:

```
self.position = ccp(newX, newY);
```

Running the game at this point should cause the unit you drag to slide along with your finger. Nice, huh? Since we have a function that moves one unit, we can very easily alter it so that every unit can be moved like this.

But first, there's something you've probably noticed a while ago (or maybe just recently), and that's the unit movement being canceled only when you bring your finger back to the original touch down position. Because we're dragging the unit itself, we can "cancel" the move by dragging the unit back to where it started. However, the finger might be in a completely different position, so we need to modify how the cancelling gets determined.

To do that, in your `touchEnded` method of `Unit.m`, locate this if statement:

```
if (ccpDistance(touchPos, self.touchDownPos) >
self.boundingBox.size.width/2)
```

Change it to the following, which will determine the unit's distance, and not the finger's distance:

```
CGPoint oldSelfPos = [MainScene
getPositionForGridCoord:self.gridPos];

CGFloat dist = ccpDistance(oldSelfPos, self.position);
if (dist > self.gridWidth/2)
```

Yes, this means you no longer need the `touchPos` variable in `touchEnded` if you're getting that warning and wish to get rid of it. But that's it for sliding 1 unit. Now we're ready to slide all the units, so let's do it!

Sliding all units

Now that we have the dragging unit being slid, let's continue and make all the units slide (even the enemy units so that we can better predict our troops' movement).

First, we need a way to move all the units on the screen. However, since the Unit class only contains information about the individual unit (which is a good thing), we need to call a method in `MainScene`, since that's where the arrays of units are.

Moreover, we cannot simply call `[MainScene method]`, since the arrays are instance variables, and instance variables must be accessed through an instance of the object itself.

That being said, because we know that our unit will be added to the scene as a child, we can use Cocos2d to our advantage, and call an instance method on the `MainScene` class via the parent parameter. So, in `touchMoved` of `Unit.m`, make the following change:

```
[(MainScene*)self.parent slideAllUnitsWithDistance:dist
withDragDirection:self.dragDirection];
```

```
//[self slideUnitWithDistance:dist
withDragDirection:self.dragDirection];
```

Basically we've commented out (or deleted) the old method call here, and instead called it on our parent object (which we cast as a `MainScene` so that we know which functions it has).

But we don't have that method created yet, so in `MainScene.h`, add the following method declaration:

```
-(void)slideAllUnitsWithDistance:(CGFloat)dist
withDragDirection:(enum UnitDirection)dir;
```

Just in case you haven't noticed, the enum UnitDirection is declared in `Unit.h`, which is why `MainScene.h` imports `Unit.h`—so that we can make use of that enum in this class, and the function to be more specific.

Then in `MainScene.m`, we're going to loop through both the friendly and enemy arrays, and call the `slideUnitWithDistance` function on each individual unit:

```
-(void)slideAllUnitsWithDistance:(CGFloat)dist
withDragDirection:(enum UnitDirection)dir
{
  for (Unit *u in arrFriendlies)
    [u slideUnitWithDistance:dist withDragDirection:dir];

  for (Unit *u in arrEnemies)
    [u slideUnitWithDistance:dist withDragDirection:dir];
}
```

However, that still isn't functional, as we haven't declared that function in the header file for the `Unit` class. So go ahead and do that now. Declare the function header in `Unit.h`:

```
-(void)slideUnitWithDistance:(CGFloat)dist withDragDirection:(enum
UnitDirection)dir;
```

We're almost done.

We initially set up our `slideUnitWithDistance` method with a drag direction in mind. However, only the unit that's currently being dragged will have a drag direction. Every other unit will need to use the direction it's currently facing (that is, the direction in which it's already going).

To do that, we just need to modify how the `slideUnitWithDistance` method does its checking to determine which direction to modify the distance by.

But first, we need to handle the negatives. What does that mean? Well, if you're dragging a unit to the left and a unit being moved is supposed to be moving to the left, it will work properly, as x-10 (for example) will still be less than the grid's width. However, if you're dragging left and a unit being moved is supposed to be moving right, it won't be moving at all, as it tries to add a negative value x -10, but because it needs to be moving to the right, it'll encounter the left-bound right away (of less than the original position), and stay still.

The following diagram should help explain what is meant by "handling negatives." As you can see, in the top section, when the non-dragged unit is supposed to be going left by 10 (in other words, negative 10 in the *x* direction), it works. But when the non-dragged unit is going the opposite sign (in other words, positive 10 in the *x* direction), it doesn't.

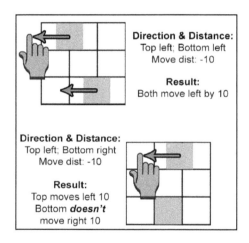

To handle this, we set up a pretty complicated if statement. It checks when the drag direction and the unit's own direction are opposite (positive versus negative), and multiplies the distance by -1 (flips it).

Add this to the top of the `slideUnitWithDistance` method, right after you grab the `newX` and the original position:

```
- (void)slideUnitWithDistance:(CGFloat)dist withDragDirection:(enum
UnitDirection)dir
{
  CGFloat newX = self.position.x, newY = self.position.y;
  CGPoint originalPos = [MainScene getPositionForGridCoord:self.
gridPos];


  if (!self.isBeingDragged &&

  (((self.direction == DirUp || self.direction == DirRight) &&
  (dir == DirDown || dir == DirLeft)) ||

  ((self.direction == DirDown || self.direction == DirLeft) &&
  (dir == DirUp || dir == DirRight))))
  {
      dist *= -1;
  }
}
```

The logic of this if statement works is as follows:

Suppose the unit is not being dragged. Also suppose that either the direction is positive and the drag direction is negative, or the direction is negative and the drag direction is positive. Then multiply by `-1`.

Finally, as mentioned earlier, we just need to handle the non-dragged units. So, in every `if` statement, add an "or" portion that will check for the same direction, but only if the unit is not currently being dragged. In other words, in the `slideUnitWithDistance` method, modify your if statements to look like this:

```
if (self.dragDirection == DirUp || (!self.isBeingDragged && self.
direction == DirUp))
{}
else if (self.dragDirection == DirDown || (!self.isBeingDragged &&
self.direction == DirDown))
{}
else if (self.dragDirection == DirLeft || (!self.isBeingDragged &&
self.direction == DirLeft))
{}
else if (self.dragDirection == DirRight || (!self.isBeingDragged &&
self.direction == DirRight))
{}
```

Finally, we can run the game. Bam! All the units go gliding across the screen with our drag. Isn't it lovely? Now the player can better choose their move.

That's it for the sliding portion (as well as this project's portion of the chapter). The rest of this chapter is filled with some really amazing things, and you're encouraged to check them out, as they may be helpful to you in your current projects outside this book, or in a future project of your own.

[The key to unit sliding is to loop through the arrays to ensure that all the units get moved by an equal amount, hence passing the distance to the move function.]

Creating movements on a Bézier curve

If you don't know what a Bézier curve is, it's basically a line that goes from point A to point B over a curve. Instead of being a straight line with two points, it uses a second set of points called control points that bend the line in a smooth way. When you want to apply movement with animations in Cocos2d, it's very tempting to queue up a bunch of MoveTo actions in a sequence. However, it's going to look a lot nicer (in both the game and the code) if you use a smoother Bézier curve animation.

Here's a good example of what a Bézier curve looks like:

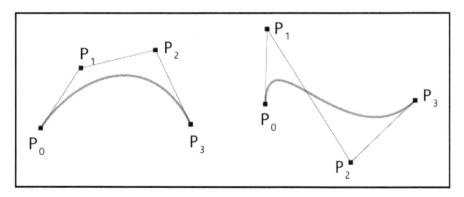

As you can see, the red line goes from point P0 to P3. However, the line is influenced in the direction of the control points, P1 and P2.

Examples of using a Bézier curve

Let's list a few examples where it would be a good choice to use a Bézier curve instead of just the regular MoveTo or MoveBy actions:

- A character that will perform a jumping animation, for example, in *Super Mario Bros*
- A boomerang as a weapon that the player throws
- Launching a missile or rocket and giving it a parabolic curve
- A tutorial hand that indicates a curved path the user must make with their finger
- A skateboarder on a half-pipe ramp (if not done with Chipmunk)

There are obviously a lot of other examples that could use a Bézier curve for their movement. But let's actually code one, shall we?

Sample project – Bézier map route

First, to make things go a lot faster—as this isn't going to be part of the book's project—simply download the project from the code repository or the website.

If you open the project and run it on your device or a simulator, you will notice a blue screen and a square in the bottom-left corner. If you tap anywhere on the screen, you'll see the blue square make an **M** shape ending in the bottom-right corner. If you hold your finger, it will repeat. Tap again and the animation will reset.

Imagine the path this square takes is over a map, and indicates what route a player will travel with their character. This is a very choppy, very sharp path. Generally, paths are curved, so let's make one that is!

Here's the end result (tracked using the CCMotionStreak method described in the *Three ways to make unit streamers or "ghosts"* section of this chapter).

Here is a screenshot that shows a very straight path of the blue square:

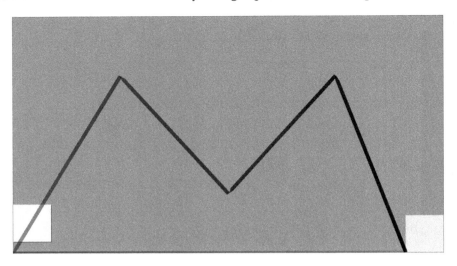

The following screenshot shows the Bézier path of the yellow square:

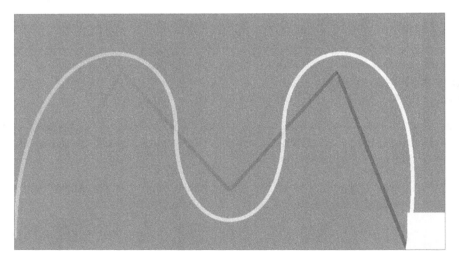

Curved M-shape

Open `MainScene.h` and add another `CCNodeColor` variable, named `unitBezier`:

```
CCNodeColor *unitBezier;
```

Then open `MainScene.m` and add the following code to the init method so that your yellow block shows up on the screen:

```
unitBezier = [[CCNodeColor alloc] initWithColor:[CCColor
colorWithRed:1 green:1 blue:0] width:50 height:50];
[self addChild:unitBezier];
CCNodeColor *shadow2 = [[CCNodeColor alloc] initWithColor:[CCColor
blackColor] width:50 height:50];
shadow2.anchorPoint = ccp(0.5,0.5);
shadow2.position = ccp(26,24);
shadow2.opacity = 0.5;
[unitBezier addChild:shadow2 z:-1];
```

Then, in the `sendFirstUnit` method, add the lines of code that will reset the yellow block's position as well as queue up the method to move the yellow block:

```
-(void)sendFirstUnit
{
  unitRegular.position = ccp(0,0);

  //Add these 2 lines
  unitBezier.position = ccp(0,0);
  [self scheduleOnce:@selector(sendSecondUnit) delay:2];

  CCActionMoveTo *move1 = [CCActionMoveTo actionWithDuration:0.5
position:ccp(winSize.width/4, winSize.height * 0.75)];
  CCActionMoveTo *move2 = [CCActionMoveTo actionWithDuration:0.5
position:ccp(winSize.width/2, winSize.height/4)];
  CCActionMoveTo *move3 = [CCActionMoveTo actionWithDuration:0.5
position:ccp(winSize.width*3/4, winSize.height * 0.75)];
  CCActionMoveTo *move4 = [CCActionMoveTo actionWithDuration:0.5
position:ccp(winSize.width - 50, 0)];

  [unitRegular runAction:[CCActionSequence actions:move1, move2,
move3, move4, nil]];
}
```

After this, you'll need to actually create the `sendSecondUnit` method, like this:

```
-(void)sendSecondUnit
{
  ccBezierConfig bezConfig1;
  bezConfig1.controlPoint_1 = ccp(0, winSize.height);
  bezConfig1.controlPoint_2 = ccp(winSize.width*3/8,
winSize.height);
  bezConfig1.endPosition = ccp(winSize.width*3/8,
winSize.height/2);
  CCActionBezierTo *bez1 = [CCActionBezierTo
actionWithDuration:1.0 bezier:bezConfig1];

  ccBezierConfig bezConfig2;
  bezConfig2.controlPoint_1 = ccp(winSize.width*3/8, 0);
  bezConfig2.controlPoint_2 = ccp(winSize.width*5/8, 0);
  bezConfig2.endPosition = ccp(winSize.width*5/8, winSize.height/2);
  CCActionBezierBy *bez2 = [CCActionBezierTo
actionWithDuration:1.0 bezier:bezConfig2];

  ccBezierConfig bezConfig3;
  bezConfig3.controlPoint_1 = ccp(winSize.width*5/8,
winSize.height);
  bezConfig3.controlPoint_2 = ccp(winSize.width, winSize.height);
  bezConfig3.endPosition = ccp(winSize.width - 50, 0);
  CCActionBezierTo *bez3 = [CCActionBezierTo
actionWithDuration:1.0 bezier:bezConfig3];

  [unitBezier runAction:[CCActionSequence actions:bez1, bez2,
bez3, nil]];
}
```

The preceding method creates three Bézier configurations and attaches them to a `MoveTo` command that takes a Bézier configuration. The reason for this is that each Bézier configuration can take only two control points. As you can see in this marked-up screenshot, where each white and red square represents a control point, you can make only a U-shaped parabola with a single Bézier configuration.

Thus, to make three U-shapes, you need three Bézier configurations.

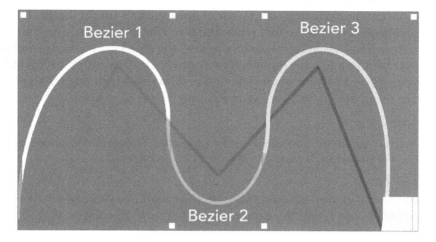

Finally, make sure that in the `touchBegan` method, you make the `unitBezier` stop all its actions (that is, stop on reset):

```
[unitBezier stopAllActions];
```

And that's it! When you run the project and tap on the screen (or tap and hold), you'll see the blue square M-shape its way across, followed by the yellow square in its squiggly M-shape.

If you want to adapt the Bézier `MoveTo` or `MoveBy` actions for your own project, you should know that you can create only one U-shape with each Bézier configuration. They're fairly easy to implement and can quickly be copied and pasted, as shown in the `sendSecondUnit` function.

Plus, as the control points and end position are just `CGPoint` values, they can be relative (that is, relative to the unit's current position, the world's position, or an enemy's position), and as a regular `CCAction`, they can be run with any `CCNode` object quite easily.

Depth perception via device tilting

Something that can increase the cool factor of your game without really changing the game is a depth-perception-like feel when the user tilts the device. This can be seen in games such as *Shadowmatic* and *Jump! Chump!*, the checklist *Wunderlist*, or a lock screen background image with **Perspective Zoom** set to **On**. Although it's subtle, it can make your game feel a lot more polished and increase user engagement, as it's just one more thing they'll find cool or interesting about the game.

 As a reminder, you cannot make use of device tilting/accelerometer in the simulator. It must be done on a physical device.

Here is *Shadowmatic* game's tilt effect seen on the menu. As you can see, it's a three-dimensional object, and the camera rotates around the object, as well as the shadows.

The first one is as follows:

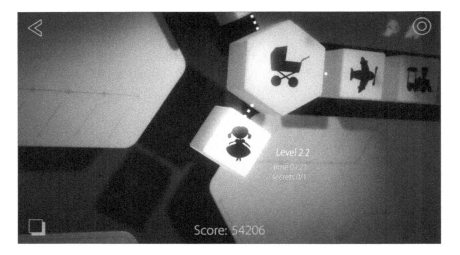

The second one is as follows:

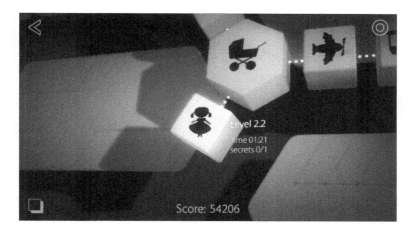

The following is *Jump! Chump!* game's tilt effect seen in the game, where you can see the shadows of the main characters and enemies being shifted.

The first one is as follows:

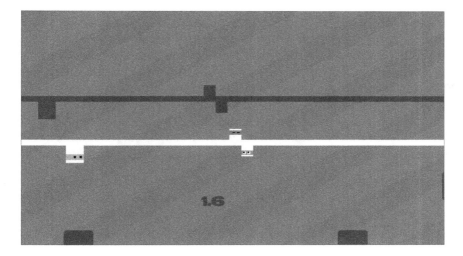

The second one is as follows:

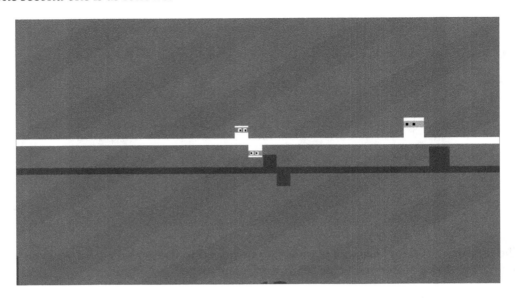

Isn't this parallax scrolling?

This is similar, but slightly different from parallax scrolling. Parallax scrolling—if you're unfamiliar—is when there are multiple background layers and each moves across the screen at a different rate to create the feeling of a more realistic movement. Cocos2d even has something called CCParallaxNode, which basically allows different relative movement speeds among the node's children. As an example, suppose you add a background image, a middle-ground image, and a foreground image with different ratios. When you move the CCParallaxNode object, it will automatically move the children as per the ratio set by each individual child.

Parallax scrolling is similar because there will still be multiple layers moving around, and they will be moving slightly in one direction or another based on the tilt of the device. Thus, the user feels as if there are objects (buttons, for example) that are literally in front of others (the grass in the background, for example).

Let's begin implementing some simple depth perception effects.

Sample project – depth

Download the Depth sample project from the code repository and run the project. You'll notice there are some background mountains, grass, and a few buttons that don't go anywhere. We're going to change this so that the buttons move around the screen to give a bit of depth.

Creating the parallax node and adding the objects

In MainScene.h, add the the variables listed here, as well as import the CoreMotion framework:

```
#import <CoreMotion/CoreMotion.h>
@interface MainScene : CCNode
{
  CGSize winSize;

  //add these
  CCParallaxNode *parallax;
  CMMotionManager *motionManager;
  CGFloat xFiltered, yFiltered ;yFiltered
}
```

The CCParallaxNode is obvious. The motionManager is meant for tracking the accelerometer data, and xFiltered and yFiltered are going to be used as filters for the accelerometer so that it doesn't become too jittery.

Now, in the init method of MainScene.m, comment out the line that adds the layoutbox to the scene. Add the code that initializes the parallax node, adds the layoutbox to it, and adds the parallax node to the scene:

```
//[self addChild:layout];

parallax = [CCParallaxNode node];
//Ratio: For every 1 pixel moved, move the child that amount
parallax.position = ccp(winSize.width/2, winSize.height/2);
[parallax addChild:layout z:0 parallaxRatio:ccp(1,1)
positionOffset:ccp(0,0)];
[self addChild:parallax];
```

If you're wondering what the ratio parameter is, it's like what the comment says: for every one pixel that the parallax object is moved, it will move the child by that amount. For example, if the parallax node was moved 100 pixels to the left, and if the child has a ratio of 0.5, the child will move to the left by 50 pixels. Does this make sense? So, for our buttons, we want the ratio to be 1:1. This means that, for every pixel the parallax node moves, the buttons will move by the same amount.

Running the project now won't do anything, however, so let's get the accelerometer data going so that we can shift the menu buttons by tilting the device.

Visualizing the depth

In the init method of `MainScene.m`, add the following block of code, which will set up the motion manager so that it can start collecting accelerometer data:

```
//60 times per second. In theory once per frame
CGFloat interval = 1/60.f;
motionManager = [[CMMotionManager alloc] init];
motionManager.accelerometerUpdateInterval = interval;
[motionManager startAccelerometerUpdates];
[self schedule:@selector(getAccelerometerData:) interval:interval];
```

For the accelerometer to affect the parallax node's position, we must create the `getAccelerometerData` method, and modify the position there:

```
- (void)getAccelerometerData:(CCTime)delta
{
   CMAcceleration accel =
motionManager.accelerometerData.acceleration;

   CGFloat filterValue  = 0.8f;

   xFiltered = filterValue * xFiltered + (1.0 - filterValue) *
accel.x;
   yFiltered = filterValue * yFiltered + (1.0 - filterValue) *
accel.y;

   parallax.position = ccp(winSize.width/2 + 50 * yFiltered,
winSize.height/2 - 50 * xFiltered);
}
```

This method basically reads the accelerometer's data 60 times per second, sends it through a filter (if you want steadier movement, increase the K value, which we called `filterValue` in the preceding code, up to a maximum of 1), and assigns the parallax's position based on the filtered *x* and *y* values.

 If this is the entirety of the effect you want in your own project, feel free to stop here. The key thing to note if you're using this in your own project is the fact that the parallax node affects every child's position based on the ratio it was given. Plus, if you're using the tilt mechanic, make sure you put a filter on the accelerometer data, or else it will be very jittery and actually hurt your game instead of helping it.

Next, we're going to equalize the parallax node so that the buttons aren't always being pushed up or off to the side.

Restoring equilibrium (calibrating to the new rotation)

After the user adjusts their phone to a new position, you would want to slowly bring their equilibrium to the way they're holding the device. For example, if they start with the device flat on a table, and then tilt it towards themselves by about 45 degrees, you will shift the items as necessary. You'll then need to slowly make the 45-degree position look the same as it did when it was flat.

This is easy to do, as long as we have a variable to hold what the equilibrium is. To do so, open `MainScene.h` and add the following code:

```
CGFloat avgXValue, avgYValue;
```

These two values will store the average of the last 100 `xFiltered` and `yFiltered` values recorded.

Then in `MainScene.m`, modify the three relevant lines in your `getAccelerometerData` method to look like what you see here:

```
avgXValue = (avgXValue * 99 + xFiltered)/100.f;
avgYValue = (avgYValue * 99 + yFiltered)/100.f;

parallax.position = ccp(winSize.width/2 + 50 * (yFiltered -
avgYValue), winSize.height/2 - 50 * (xFiltered - avgXValue));
```

At first, the math probably makes no sense, so let's go over it.

First, avgXValue and avgYValue calculate the average by slowly adding one point at a time to the average in an estimation sort of way. This is not 100 percent accurate in the true "average" sense, but it comes close enough. It's also slightly better to do it this way as it means less code, less memory, and faster execution. Since we're doing this 60 times per second, it's not entirely important to get an accurate average. Within a few seconds, you'll have hundreds of points that will get you close enough.

Second, the subtraction of xFiltered/xFiltered and avgYValue/avgXValue is done to slowly bring it back to the center. For example, if your yFiltered value is -1, and avgYValue is 0, it will quickly jump down to its new position. But if the device is held at -1 for long enough, avgYValue will come so close to -1 that subtracting the two variables will yield a zeroed-out position, which is exactly what we want.

The key thing to note here if you are implementing the calibration effect into your own project is to subtract the two values. Whether you use a single-value calibration or a pseudo-average value (like what was used here), if you don't subtract the filtered *x* and *y* values, you won't see any change.

For slow calibration, the preceding method is the way to go. If you want instant calibration (for example, with a button that realigns when the user says so), simply store the single accelerometer value when the button is pressed rather than store the average value.

A quick scrolling example

Since we're covering the topic of parallax scrolling, let's quickly go over a simple example of parallax scrolling as it was intended. In MainScene.m (or the header; it doesn't really matter), import the GameScene.h file:

```
#import "GameScene.h"
```

Then, in the buttonPressed method, add the following line of code. It will go to the game scene:

```
[[CCDirector sharedDirector] replaceScene:[GameScene scene]];
```

Now let's add the CCParallaxNode to GameScene.h:

```
@interface GameScene : CCScene
{
  CGSize winSize;

  //add this:
  CCParallaxNode *parallax;
}
```

Then, in the GameScene.m file's init method, set up the parallax node and add a few sprites to the node:

```
CCSprite *bg1 = [CCSprite spriteWithImageNamed:@"mountains.png"];
CCSprite *bg2 = [CCSprite spriteWithImageNamed:@"mountains.png"];

CCSprite *mg1 = [CCSprite spriteWithImageNamed:@"midground.png"];
CCSprite *mg2 = [CCSprite spriteWithImageNamed:@"midground.png"];

CCSprite *fg1 = [CCSprite spriteWithImageNamed:@"foreground.png"];
CCSprite *fg2 = [CCSprite spriteWithImageNamed:@"foreground.png"];
fg1.anchorPoint = fg2.anchorPoint = ccp(0.5,0);

CCSprite *sun = [CCSprite spriteWithImageNamed:@"sun.png"];

parallax = [CCParallaxNode node];
parallax.anchorPoint = ccp(0,0);
parallax.position = ccp(0,0);

[parallax addChild:bg1 z:0 parallaxRatio:ccp(0.35,0)
positionOffset:ccp(winSize.width/2, winSize.height/2)];

[parallax addChild:bg2 z:0 parallaxRatio:ccp(0.35,0)
positionOffset:ccp(winSize.width/2 + winSize.width - 2,winSize.
height/2)];

[parallax addChild:sun z:1 parallaxRatio:ccp(0.5,0)
positionOffset:ccp(winSize.width, winSize.height * 0.8)];

[parallax addChild:mg1 z:1 parallaxRatio:ccp(0.5,0)
positionOffset:ccp(winSize.width/2, winSize.height/2)];
```

```
[parallax addChild:mg2 z:1 parallaxRatio:ccp(0.5,0)
positionOffset:ccp(winSize.width/2 + winSize.width, winSize.
height/2)];

[parallax addChild:fg1 z:2 parallaxRatio:ccp(1,0)
positionOffset:ccp(winSize.width/2, 0)];

[parallax addChild:fg2 z:2 parallaxRatio:ccp(1,0)
positionOffset:ccp(winSize.width/2 + winSize.width, 0)];

[self addChild:parallax];
```

Just in case you're wondering what `positionOffset` does, it moves the node to the position given as a parameter before any parallax ratios get applied. This is useful when first setting up your scene (just as we're doing here).

Then, we want to enable touching, so we add this line to the `init` method:

```
[self setUserInteractionEnabled:YES];
```

But first, we need to create a variable to hold the previous position the finger was at so that we know how far to move the parallax node. Therefore, in `GameScene.h`, add the following:

```
CGPoint previousPosition;
```

Finally, add the `touchBegan` and `touchMoved` methods so that the parallax node moves according to the `touchMoved` distance, while also making sure that the scrolling never goes beyond the bounds:

```
-(void)touchBegan:(CCTouch *)touch withEvent:(CCTouchEvent *)event
{
    previousPosition = [touch locationInNode:self];
}

-(void)touchMoved:(CCTouch *)touch withEvent:(CCTouchEvent *)event
{
    CGPoint newPosition = [touch locationInNode:self];

    parallax.position = ccp(parallax.position.x + (newPosition.x -
previousPosition.x), 0);
```

```
    if (parallax.position.x < -winSize.width)
        parallax.position = ccp(-winSize.width,0);
    if (parallax.position.x > 0)
        parallax.position = ccp(0,0);

    previousPosition = newPosition;
}
```

From here onwards, you can run the project, and when you click on **Play**, you'll be taken to the game scene, which now has a (rather crude) set of background, middle-ground, and foreground elements. When you drag your finger across the screen, you'll notice the grass scrolling at the same speed while the mountains, trees, and sun all scroll at different speeds.

 If you're implementing a parallax scrolling background in your own project, the key thing to note is the difference in ratios between the added objects. Once you have that squared away, all you have to do is move the parallax node with respect to a finger dragging, a character moving, or whatever.

Three ways to make unit streamers or "ghosts"

If you've ever played games such as *Fruit Ninja, Blek, Jetpack Joyride,* or *Tiny Wings,* you've surely seen this effect. There's a position on the screen that generates something similar to stars, a slashing effect, smoke clouds, or a line following the finger.

Sample project – ghosts

Go to the code repository and open the `Ghosts` project under the `Sample Projects` folder. If you run it, you will see just three labels as buttons that lead to mostly blank screens that don't really do anything. That's where you come in.

Here, you're going to learn how to make the effects that you just read. There are three general ways to go about making something like this. Let's go over each method, starting with the easiest and ending with the hardest.

Method 1 – particle systems

Particle systems are basically sprites that are created en masse, such as a firework effect, a gushing water fountain, or a flickering candle. The difference between using a particle system and creating the sprites yourself is that particle systems generally allow only moving, scaling, rotation, and color changes. But for simple effects such as a smoke cloud, a particle system works just fine.

 If you wish to create your own particles for this sample project or any project of your own, as mentioned in *Chapter 1, Refreshing Your Cocos2d Knowledge*, Particle Designer is a great tool for this purpose. You can manually create them in the code, but it's a lot easier and more efficient to create them visually using an editor such as Particle Designer.

With the `Ghosts` project opened in Xcode, open the `ParticleExampleScene.h` file and add a `CCParticleSystem` variable to the list:

```
CCParticleSystem *smokeParticle;
```

Then open `ParticleExampleScene.m` and add the particle system to the screen in the init method:

```
smokeParticle = [CCParticleSystem

  particleWithFile:@"SmokeParticle.plist"];

[self addChild:smokeParticle];
```

The particle system used in the preceding code was created using Particle Designer, as mentioned at the beginning of this book. It uses a simple cloud-shaped image and has certain properties set to create the effect of fading out.

Finally, in the `updateParticleSource` method, set the particle system's source position so that as you drag your finger around the screen, the smoke starts in a different position:

```
smokeParticle.sourcePosition = startPosition;
```

If you run the project at this point, you'll see that the smoke is constantly being generated, even after you take your finger off the screen. Although this doesn't mean much for this sample project, imagine you want a particle being displayed only if a user is in midair, or while a combo move is being performed. That being said, we need a way to stop and start the particle streaming on demand (in this case, when the user places or removes their finger).

Although Cocos2d does not have a method to begin a particle system, it's very easy to add such a method. So, look up the project for stopSystem. In the CCParticleSystemBase.h file (which should be the first result in the search), add the following code above the stopSystem declaration:

```
-(void) startSystem;
```

Then, in the CCParticleSystemBase.m file (the next result in the search), add this method so that you can start the particle system on demand:

```
-(void) startSystem
{
  _active = YES;
  _elapsed = _duration;
  _emitCounter = 0;
}
```

Now go back to ParticleExampleScene.m, and in the init method, right after you've added the smoke particle to the scene, call the stopSystem method so that it's not on the screen when the scene first starts:

```
[smokeParticle stopSystem];
```

Add the stopSystem method to the touchEnded method so that the particle system stops spawning new particles and lets the old particles die out:

```
-(void) touchEnded:(CCTouch *)touch withEvent:(CCTouchEvent *)event
{
    isStreaming = NO;
    [smokeParticle stopSystem];
}
```

Finally, add a method call to the newly created startSystem method in the touchBegan method so that the particles begin streaming when a finger is on the screen:

```
[smokeParticle startSystem];
```

Running the project at this point will allow you to see the starting and stopping of a particle system that has already been created.

You may be wondering how to adapt this for your own project. Once you have the particle system added to the screen, it's basically just a matter of updating the particle system's source position with the "start position." For example, you could have a rocket flying across the screen, and the rocket's position could be the start position.

Now let's move on to a very similar-looking style that takes a little more code, but allows greater manipulation with the overall look of the game.

Method 2 – sprites or nodes

Although a particle system requires less code to get a similar effect, there are more things you can do when you create the sprite yourself and handle everything that happens to it. For example, you can make the sprite change color several times, set up crazy movement patterns, change images altogether, or apply other CCAction actions that the particle system can't do.

One example of something that a particle system can't do is shake mechanics. A simple way you can do this is by queuing up a sequence of CCMove actions to go in the various directions you want (generally, no more than a few points in any direction), and using a variable for the duration so that you can increase or decrease the speed based on the situation.

With the Ghosts project opened in Xcode, open the SpriteExampleScene.m file and add the following block of code to the spawnStreamer method:

```
CCSprite *heart = [CCSprite spriteWithImageNamed:@"heart.png"];
heart.color = [CCColor redColor];
heart.position = startPosition;
[self addChild:heart];

CCActionScaleTo *shrink = [CCActionScaleTo actionWithDuration:0.5
scale:0];
CCActionCallBlock *block = [CCActionCallBlock actionWithBlock:^{
  [self removeChild:heart];
}];

[heart runAction:[CCActionSequence actions:shrink, block, nil]];
```

This code will spawn a red heart (the image is white, but we've colored it red), shrink it down to a scale of 0 in half a second, and then remove it from the scene so that it doesn't create lag after running for a while.

If you run the project and drag you finger around the screen, you'll see some beautiful hearts being created in a fluid manner. And that's it! The only reason it was mentioned that you'd probably have to use more code is that, the more you want to do with your streamer (ghost, phantom, or whatever), the more code it will take to get the effect you want.

So say, for example, you want to make the sprites move along a Bézier curve, spin 360 degrees, and finally shrink down and disappear, while at the same time changing to a green heart. The code will look something like this:

```
CCSprite *heart = [CCSprite spriteWithImageNamed:@"heart.png"];
heart.color = [CCColor redColor];
heart.position = startPosition;
[self addChild:heart];

CCActionTintTo *tint = [CCActionTintTo actionWithDuration:0.5
color:[CCColor greenColor]];

ccBézierConfig bezConfig;
bezConfig.controlPoint_1 = ccp(0,100);
bezConfig.controlPoint_2 = ccp(100,100);
bezConfig.endPosition = ccp(100,0);
CCActionBézierTo *move = [CCActionBézierBy actionWithDuration:0.5
Bézier:bezConfig];

CCActionRotateBy *rotate = [CCActionRotateBy actionWithDuration:0.5
angle:360];

CCActionScaleTo *shrink = [CCActionScaleTo actionWithDuration:0.5
scale:0];
CCActionCallBlock *remove = [CCActionCallBlock actionWithBlock:^{
  [self removeChild:heart];
}];

[heart runAction:tint];
[heart runAction:[CCActionSequence actions:move, rotate, shrink,
remove, nil]];
```

If you wish to implement something like this within your own project, the key requirement is the isStreaming Boolean and the check within the update method. Everything else is straightforward and very similar to the particle method of changing the startPosition.

Finally, let's tackle the most unique method of all—the constant line that both *Fruit Ninja* and *Blek* have implemented.

Method 3 – constant line

Constant line is the most advanced version of streamers. It's not really a particle, and therefore, it can't be made as a sprite creation either. Instead, we're going to use CCMotionStreak to create a slashing effect. CCMotionStreak is fairy simple to implement, as it only needs a position, an image, and a color.

With the Ghosts project opened in Xcode, open ConstantLineExampleScene.h and add a CCMotionStreak object to the list:

```
{
   CGSize winSize;
   CGPoint startPosition;

   CCMotionStreak *streak;
}
```

Then, in ConstantLineExampleScene.m, create the streak and add it to the scene in the init method:

```
streak = [CCMotionStreak streakWithFade:0.35 minSeg:1 width:15
color:[CCColor yellowColor] textureFilename:@"blade.png"];
[self addChild:streak];
```

Here we're using the yellow color and the file named blade.png. You can use whichever image you want, but since we want a blade slashing effect, we're going to use the image that is shaped like a diamond to give the beginning and end a pointed edge.

Next, in the touchBegan method, set the CCMotionStreak object's position, and reset it so that when the users touch down again, it doesn't connect the two lines (unless that's what you want; in that case, you should not reset it):

```
streak.position = startPosition;
[streak reset];
```

Finally, in the `touchMoved` method, set the position so that every time the finger is dragged, the motion streak glides to the next position:

```
streak.position = startPosition;
```

And that's it! If you run the project, go to the line example, and drag a finger around, you'll see the nice slashing effect. If you want to make the line bigger (or smaller), simply adjust the width in the initialization of `CCMotionStreak`. The same applies to the color, image, or even duration. However, it's not recommended to set the duration too high, as the motion streak might be a bit delayed.

The key point to remember if you want to implement this style of streamer/ghost in your project is that `CCMotionStreak` relies on a position of something. So, if you want a streak on a spaceship, you have to update the motion streak's position in the update function, like this:

```
-(void)update:(CCTime)delta
{
    streak.position = ship.position;
}
```

Touchscreen controls versus D-pad adaptation (and why it matters so much to know this distinction)

Because we're coding for iOS, it's important to note the uniqueness of the device we're creating games for, that is, the touchscreen itself versus a plastic controller with joysticks and triggers that the user has in their hands. When creating games for iOS (or any smartphone device with a touchscreen), you must create the controls such that they feel natural and fluid on the device, as if the game never existed on another console.

Granted, it's understandable that some games are better suited for D-pad-style movement. However, there's always the accelerometer, swipe controls, or the way that Infinity Blade does it (using small buttons on the screen to block or dodge, and also using swipes across the center of the screen to attack with your sword).

Unfortunately, there's no "how to program" section for the best controls, as it's all based on your individual game. For example, in this book's game, we don't tap a unit and then use a D-pad to tell the game which direction to send the unit in. Instead, we make use of the touch-and-drag feature of iOS and integrate that as part of our controls.

There are more good examples of touch-integrated controls later in this chapter, but first, let's go over what not to do.

Bad examples of iOS game controls

The following are some examples of some games that just basically took the controls they had on their console or PC version of the game and dumped them into the touchscreen, hoping it would work out for them.

Game Dev Story: Although this is not a bad game on its own, the controls are completely menu driven and don't feel as if they were created with a mobile in mind.

Tomb Raider I: Just based on the screenshots, it's easy to see how complex the controls are and how little time the developers put into innovating their control scheme for the mobile platform.

Duke Nukem 3D: Again, just based on the following screenshot, you can understand what bad controls are being pointed out here:

Midway Arcade: They could've done so much better when it comes to cycling through the mini-games and even the mini-games themselves. Some of the games feel mobile friendly, but the rest are just not pulling their weight.

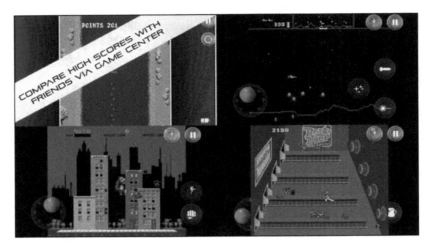

Great examples of touchscreen controls

In this section, you'll find some games that, whether they started on console before or not, have some great controls on mobile. They exhibit everything beautiful about being able to code games for a handheld device with a touchscreen and an accelerometer.

First up is *Shadowmatic*; you drag the screen to rotate the objects, and tilting the device moves the camera so slightly that you really get a three-dimension-like feeling in this game.

Next is *Smash Hit*; not only does it spawn the metal balls where your finger touches but also the easy-to-press buttons cause no disruptions to the gameplay either.

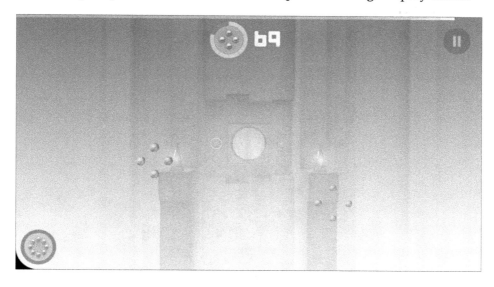

I can't forget *Angry Birds*, with its pinch-zoom, pullback mechanics, and easy-to-understand gameplay, all of which stem from great touchscreen controls.

There's also *Temple Run*, integrating the swiping mechanics in every direction, making the user feel as if they're actually pushing their character in the particular direction.

Last but not least (as there are surely a lot more that also have great touchscreen controls) is *Blek*. I'm not even sure whether this game could exist outside a touchscreen environment because it's just so fluid!

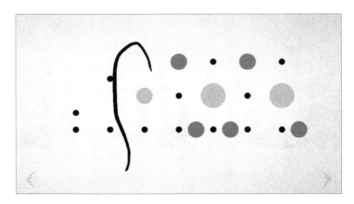

Summary

In this chapter, you learned how to do a variety of things, from making a score table and previewing the next move, to making use of Bézier curves and creating unit streamers.

Remember, if you ever need to come back to this chapter (or any other for that matter), don't hesitate to do so. The code was built with a copy-paste mindset, so it can be adapted for any project without much reworking (if it is required at all).

In the next chapter, we will enhance this game, which used only programmer art until now, so that it looks like something a team of 20 people spent months developing.

6
Tidying Up and Polishing

Polishing is the most important thing you'll learn in this entire book. If you can master the art of making your game polished, it doesn't matter how simple or complex it is; you'll have a great game. And yes, even though you may be a great programmer who hasn't had a bug in your program in years, or an artist who makes people faint when they see your character designs, you still need to polish you game. It's absolutely necessary for any modern game to be a solid experience for the player.

In this chapter, you'll learn what it takes to clean up the game, smooth out the rough edges, and turn that game with cool mechanics into a fun, playable, and unforgettable experience. But it's not just about making it look good. It needs to feel good, and the entire user experience needs to be joyful. In no particular order, we will cover the following:

- Button press visual
- Pulse on unit combine
- A tutorial
- Sharing over Facebook and Twitter (and more)
- Sound on/off
- Game Center leaderboards
- Slide transitions

Obviously, you don't have to do all of these, but if you want more people to play your game, chances are that they're more likely to play it if it's polished. Now, the biggest thing when it comes to polishing is the graphical and sound styles. They need to be consistent throughout, as well as visually appealing so that the user doesn't get confused or put off when they play your game.

That being said, if you open the Chapter 6 project, you'll see that the game's graphics and fonts have been updated. It looks and feels pretty solid. The only thing left to do is what's being covered in this chapter (as you just saw in the list). So let's get to it.

Button press visuals

Yeah, button press visuals are great! Cocos2d is nice enough to provide a darkening of the button when we touch it, but let's add a bit more animation to our buttons to give them more of that "clicked" feeling.

Modifying the CCButton class

If we just wanted an individual button to have a specific effect, we would modify just that single button in the place where it exists. However, we want the same button effect across all buttons in our game, so we need to open CCButton.m file. The easiest way to do that is to search for CCButton in the project and click on any of the links to CCButton.m.

Here, you're going to add two functions near the top of the file: scaleButtonUp and scaleButtonDown. Both of them run actions on the button, and these actions give it a bouncy press effect found in many games:

 Alternatively, you can extend/subclass CCButton and override the methods necessary to create the desired effect. This method is also slightly more stable in the case of a Cocos2d version update that changes the default code of CCButton. But for now, we'll just modify the existing CCButton code.

```
@implementation CCButton

//add this one...
-(void)scaleButtonDown
{
  [self stopAllActions];

  id scaleDown = [CCActionEaseInOut actionWithAction:
  [CCActionScaleTo actionWithDuration:0.11f scale:0.8f] rate:2];
  id scaleBackUp = [CCActionEaseInOut actionWithAction:
  [CCActionScaleTo actionWithDuration:0.13f scale:0.9f] rate:2];
  id actionSequence = [CCActionSequence actions:scaleDown,
  scaleBackUp, nil];
  [self runAction:actionSequence];
```

```
}

//and this one...
-(void)scaleButtonUp
{
  [self stopAllActions];

  id scaleDown = [CCActionEaseInOut actionWithAction:
    [CCActionScaleTo actionWithDuration:0.11f scale:1.15f]
    rate:1.5f];
  id scaleBackUp = [CCActionEaseInOut actionWithAction:
    [CCActionScaleTo actionWithDuration:0.13f scale:1.0f] rate:2];
  id actionSequence = [CCActionSequence actions:scaleDown,
    scaleBackUp, nil];
  [self runAction:actionSequence];
}
```

Then at the bottom of the `touchEntered` method, add the call to the
`scaleButtonDown` method like so:

```
- (void) touchEntered:(CCTouch *)touch withEvent:(CCTouchEvent
  *)event
{

  ...

  //add this:
  [self scaleButtonDown];
}
```

Finally, in `touchExited` and `touchUpInside`, you have to add the call to the
`scaleButtonUp` methods. This is meant for the following cases: either when the
players, finger leaves the button (indicating that it won't be activated if they lift
their finger), or when they actually "press" the button:

```
- (void) touchExited:(CCTouch *)touch withEvent:(CCTouchEvent
  *)event
{
  self.highlighted = NO;

  //add this:
  [self scaleButtonUp];
}

- (void) touchUpInside:(CCTouch *)touch withEvent:(CCTouchEvent
  *)event
{
```

```
    . . .

    //add this:
    [self scaleButtonUp];
}
```

And that's it! It took a whole 2 minutes to add that extra bit of polishing to our buttons. It's not something that's going to sell the game on its own, but it's subtle enough to give your players a feeling like, "Wow, the developers really took the time to make this game right!"

Pulse on unit combine

When our units combine, nothing special really happens. So, what we're going to do is add a slight pulse effect. Basically, when two units combine we want the unit to grow in a fashion similar to the button visual we just created (where it expands and then scales down again).

You can also do fancy things in general when the units spawn, such as particle effects (for example, a subtle explosion/burst effect), sprite animations, and other various things.

The key to polishing is thinking out of the box, yet looking at things you already have within the game to keep the aesthetic consistent and solid.

To carry out the pulsing we desire, since we'll most likely be placing the same code in multiple places, let's create a method that takes in a CCNode object and applies the effect we have in mind. So in MainScene.m, add the following method somewhere in the code (preferably near the combination code):

```
- (void)pulseUnit:(CCNode*)unit
{
  CGFloat baseScale = 1.0f;
  if (UI_USER_INTERFACE_IDIOM() == UIUserInterfaceIdiomPhone)
    baseScale = 0.8f;

  id scaleUp = [CCActionEaseInOut actionWithAction:[CCActionScaleTo
actionWithDuration:0.15f
  scale:baseScale * 1.2f] rate:2];
  id scaleDown = [CCActionEaseInOut actionWithAction:[CCActionScaleTo
actionWithDuration:0.15f
  scale:baseScale * 0.9f] rate:2];
```

```
    id scaleToFinal = [CCActionEaseInOut actionWithAction:[CCActionScale
To actionWithDuration:0.25f
    scale:baseScale] rate:2];
    id seq = [CCActionSequence actions:scaleUp, scaleDown,
    scaleToFinal, nil];

    [unit stopAllActions];
    [unit runAction:seq];
}
```

This function takes into consideration the "original scale" of the unit, and then runs a two-action sequence of scaling up and then down. However, we want to make sure we stop all the current actions on the unit in the case of there being more than two units that combine (and we will subsequently call this function multiple times on the same unit).

Now that we have a function ready, let's add the calls to it in the four places where a unit is combined.

The first two places are in the `checkForCombineWithUnit` method (again, if you aren't using the `Chapter 6` code here, this method isn't implemented):

```
-(void)checkForCombineWithUnit:(Unit*)first andUnit:(Unit*)other
    usingDeletionArray:(NSMutableArray*)array
{
    . . .

        if (ov > fv)
        {
            . . .

            [self pulseUnit:other];
        }
        else
        {
            . . .

            [self pulseUnit:first];
        }
    . . .
}
```

The last two places are in the `checkForAnyDirectionCombine` method:

```
- (void)checkForAnyDirectionCombineWithUnit:(Unit*)first
  andUnit:(Unit*)other usingDeletionArray:(NSMutableArray*)array
{
  ...

    if (ov > fv)
    {
      ...

      [self pulseUnit:other];
    }
    else
    {
      ...


      [self pulseUnit:first];
    }
  }
}
```

And that's it! Run the game and combine two units, and you'll see the pulsing effect. Again, it's subtle, but that's exactly what we need—many subtle changes that add up to a lot over time.

Tutorial

We're at the point where we need to teach our players how to play our game. Although you might have been able to explain the game to your testers when you were standing over their shoulders, you won't be able to do that for those who download the app from the App Store. Thus, we're in need of a tutorial, and a quick one because we want our players playing the game, not the tutorial.

For this project, we're going to have a simple tutorial that basically explains the main concepts of the game through only a few words and some images:

- Players sliding units with their fingers
- Combining their own units
- Defeating enemy units
- Protecting the central square

Obviously, we are able to go a lot more in depth by explaining a few more of the subtle concepts, but instead, we're giving the player room to learn, experiment, and test things for themselves. We just want the tutorial to set them up so that they don't get frustrated when they either don't know what to do when the game starts, or lose and don't know why they lost.

Tutorial phase variable and the NSUserDefaults key

We want to know at what point in the tutorial our user is. So, we need to know what set of text and options to display. For example, if we create a tutorial that uses multiple scenes, we wouldn't have needed a variable, as the scene would have indicated which tutorial we were on. However, because we're doing everything within the `MainScene` (and because we want to smoothly transition into a regular game after the tutorial is over), it's best to use a variable to track how far we've gone.

So (since we'll want to access the variable in a later portion), let's create an `@ property` variable in `MainScene.h`, like this:

```
}
+(CCScene*)scene;

...

//here:
@property (nonatomic, assign) NSInteger tutorialPhase;
@end
```

If it's a good tutorial, the user learns the first time they're going through it, so it's a good assumption to set a "did they finish it?" variable to true after they've gone through all the steps. This means that we want to record in a variable whether or not they've finished the tutorial before, so we're going to use `NSUserDefaults` again. Let's define another key so that we can eliminate human errors as well as increase code readability. In `MainScene.h`, declare the following key with the rest at the top of the file:

```
FOUNDATION_EXPORT NSString *const KeyFinishedTutorial;
```

In `MainScene.m`, define the key at the top, with something like the following:

```
NSString *const KeyFinishedTutorial = @"keyFinishedTutorial";
```

Finally, we want to determine whether or not to show the tutorial. Since we have this key storing the determining factor, we can simply read that from NSUserDefaults and either run the game as normal or begin the tutorial in phase 1.

So in MainScene.m, at the bottom of your init method, modify the spawnNewEnemy call to the following:

```
if ([[NSUserDefaults standardUserDefaults]
  boolForKey:KeyFinishedTutorial])
{
  [self spawnNewEnemy:[self getRandomEnemy]];
  self.tutorialPhase = 0;
}
else
{
  //spawn enemy on far right with value of 1
  Unit *newEnemy = [Unit enemyUnitWithNumber:1
    atGridPosition:ccp(9, 5)];
  newEnemy.position = [MainScene getPositionForGridCoord:
    newEnemy.gridPos];
  [newEnemy setDirection:DirLeft];
  [self spawnNewEnemy:newEnemy];
  self.tutorialPhase = 1;

  [self showTutorialInstructions];
}
```

Also, to eliminate errors and set ourselves up for easier coding later, we define the showTutorialInstructions object (the empty body is okay for now; we'll cover that next):

```
- (void)showTutorialInstructions
{
}
```

In the preceding if-else statement, you see the tutorialPhase being set to either 0 (not going through the tutorial this time) or 1 (begin the tutorial at phase 1), based on whether they've finished the tutorial or not. If they haven't, it will also spawn a new enemy at the far right with a value of 1.

That's the beginning of our tutorial—setting up the necessary structure. Next, we're going to tackle actually displaying some text, depending on what phase of the tutorial we're in.

Displaying text for each phase (and CCSprite9Slice)

Each tutorial phase needs to have its own text. To do that, we'll just reference the tutorial phase variable and assign the text to a label based on what phase we're in. That said, in the `showTutorialInstructions` method that we just created, we add the following lines to display our initial phase 1 text:

```
NSString *tutString = @"";
if (self.tutorialPhase == 1)
{
tutString = @"Drag Friendly Units";
}

CCLabelBMFont *lblTutorialText = [CCLabelBMFont
  labelWithString:tutString fntFile:@"bmScoreFont.fnt"];
lblTutorialText.color = [CCColor colorWithRed:52/255.f
  green:73/255.f blue:94/255.f];
lblTutorialText.position = [MainScene
  getPositionForGridCoord:ccp(5,2)];
lblTutorialText.name = @"tutorialText";
[self addChild:lblTutorialText z:2];
CCSprite9Slice *background = [CCSprite9Slice
  spriteWithSpriteFrame:[[CCSpriteFrameCache
  sharedSpriteFrameCache] spriteFrameByName:@"imgUnit.png"]];
background.margin = 0.2;
background.position = ccp(0.5,0.4);
background.positionType = CCPositionTypeNormalized;
background.contentSize = CGSizeMake(1.05f, 1.2f);
background.contentSizeType = CCSizeTypeNormalized;
[lblTutorialText addChild:background z:-1];
```

Run the project. You'll see the text spanning across the top center of the grid. But code-wise, there's a lot going on in the block we just added, so let's quickly go over the new stuff.

First, we're naming (a tag property in previous versions, but it's now a string) the label so that we can access the `CCNode` by searching for it later using the `getChildByName` function. Next, we're positioning the label at `z:2`, so we're ensuring that it's above everything else (the default is `z:0`, and at most, we have our units at `z:1`, so `z:2`, should be good).

There's also the `CCSprite9Slice` object, which is most likely new to you. If you've never heard of a 9-slice (or 9-patch) sprite before, refer to the following diagram to learn about it:

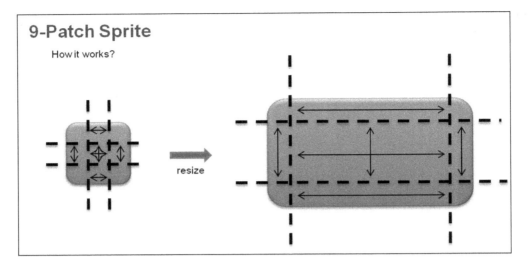

In short, the central section can scale in any direction, the corners do not scale, the top and bottom margins scale horizontally, and the left and right margins scale vertically.

You'll require the 9-slice sprite only when you want the margins to scale. In any other situation, it's better to use a regular `CCSprite`.

Since we want to keep our art style consistent, we can use `Unit.png` as our 9-slice sprite, along with a 20 percent margin (the rest is whitespace anyways, so this is a good number to go with). Then we'll position it behind the label (using `z:-1`) and set the content size to slightly larger than the width and height of the label.

When using `CCSprite9Slice`, if you want to change the `scale` of the button, you must change its `contentSize` value, *not* the scale property.

Also, the margin value (or values) can only go up to a maximum of 0.5 (which means 50 percent of the image in any direction).

Now we're actually going to take the tutorial to the next phase.

Advancing the tutorial

Just the fact that we have text displayed doesn't mean we have something impressive, as it's not really a tutorial up to this point. We need to implement the advanced portion. So, create a function called `advanceTutorial` as well as `removePreviousTutorialPhase` (which will be used to get rid of the previous phases' text) and edit them like this:

```
-(void)advanceTutorial
{
    ++self.tutorialPhase;
    [self removePreviousTutorialPhase];

    if (self.tutorialPhase<7)
    {
        [self showTutorialInstructions];
    }
    else
    {
        //the tutorial should be marked as "visible"
        [[NSUserDefaults standardUserDefaults] setBool:YES
            forKey:KeyFinishedTutorial];
        [[NSUserDefaults standardUserDefaults] synchronize];
    }
}
-(void)removePreviousTutorialPhase
{
}
```

Essentially, we're saying that if we advance to the next tutorial phase, and the phase is less than 7, we just show the next tutorial's instructions. Otherwise, we simply set the `didFinishTutorial` Boolean to `true`.

Finally, we should include the proper text for each phase so that when we start advancing the tutorial phase, we can actually see the progress. So, in the `showTutorialInstructions` function, modify the `if` statement to look like the following (which also creates and displays a **How to Play** label for the first phase):

```
if (self.tutorialPhase == 1)
{
    tutString = @"Drag Friendly Units";

    CCLabelBMFont *lblHowToPlay = [CCLabelBMFont labelWithString:@"How
to Play:" fntFile:@"bmScoreFont.fnt"];
```

```
    lblHowToPlay.color = [CCColor colorWithRed:52/255.f
      green:73/255.f blue:94/255.f];
    lblHowToPlay.position = [MainScene
      getPositionForGridCoord:ccp(5,1)];
    lblHowToPlay.name = @"lblHowToPlay";
    lblHowToPlay.scale = 0.8;
    [self addChild:lblHowToPlay z:2];

    CCSprite9Slice *bgHowTo = [CCSprite9Slice
      spriteWithSpriteFrame:[[CCSpriteFrameCache
      sharedSpriteFrameCache] spriteFrameByName:@"imgUnit.png"]];
    bgHowTo.margin = 0.2;
    bgHowTo.position = ccp(0.5,0.4);
    bgHowTo.positionType = CCPositionTypeNormalized;
    bgHowTo.contentSize = CGSizeMake(1.05f, 1.2f);
    bgHowTo.contentSizeType = CCSizeTypeNormalized;
    [lblHowToPlay addChild:bgHowTo z:-1];
}
else if (self.tutorialPhase == 2)
{
    tutString = @"Combine Friendly Units";

    id fadeRemoveHowToPlay = [CCActionSequence
      actions:[CCActionEaseInOut actionWithAction:[CCActionFadeOut
      actionWithDuration:0.5f] rate:2], [CCActionCallBlock
      actionWithBlock:^{
      [self removeChildByName:@"lblHowToPlay"];
    }], nil];

    [[self getChildByName:@"lblHowToPlay" recursively:NO]
      runAction:fadeRemoveHowToPlay];

}
else if (self.tutorialPhase == 3)
{
    tutString = @"Defeat Enemies";
}
else if (self.tutorialPhase == 4)
{
    tutString = @"Protect Center";
}
else if (self.tutorialPhase == 5)
{
```

```
    tutString = @"Survive";
}
else if (self.tutorialPhase == 6)
{
    tutString = @"Enjoy! :)";
}
```

 Note that the preceding code can also be written in the form of switch-case statements.

So that's it! Let's actually take our tutorial ahead so that we can see our progress in action as we walk through each phase.

Advancing in all the right places

Since we have all the functions laid out, all we need to do is call the `advanceTutorial` function when we want the next phase to begin.

The first phase will advance once we've moved the unit for the first time, so in the `moveUnit` function, add the following to the bottom:

```
if (self.tutorialPhase == 1 || self.tutorialPhase == 2)
    [self advanceTutorial];
```

And hey! While we're at it, we might as well include phase 2, right? After all, we're just sliding once in both phases.

Phase 3 will end when the enemy coming in from the right is destroyed, so in the `handleCollisionWithFriendly` function, you need to add the following method call within the if statement shown here. Phase 4 will also end when a unit gets destroyed, so we'll go ahead and include it as well:

```
if (enemy.unitValue<= 0)
{
    [arrEnemies removeObject:enemy];
    [selfremoveChild:enemy];
    ++numUnitsKilled;

    if (self.tutorialPhase == 3 || self.tutorialPhase == 4)
[selfadvanceTutorial];
}
```

Next is going to be when tutorial phase 5 ends, which is after the user wants to make their move but before any unit movements have been calculated. The same applies to phase 6, so add the following call to the advanceTutorial function at the top of the moveUnit function. This is because we don't want to accidentally advance the tutorial twice (which is what would happen if we add it at the bottom):

```
if (self.tutorialPhase == 5 || self.tutorialPhase == 6)
    [self advanceTutorial];
```

But hold on for a second! We want to ensure the same experience for every person in the tutorial. So, just like the way we created a custom unit at the beginning of the scene in the init method, we're going to create a custom unit in the moveUnit function. In your moveUnit function, modify this if statement to create a custom unit when you're in the corresponding tutorial phase:

```
if (numTurnSurvived % 3 == 0 || [arrEnemiescount] == 0)
{
    if (self.tutorialPhase == 4)
    {
        Unit *newEnemy = [Unit enemyUnitWithNumber:4
            atGridPosition:ccp(5,9)];
        [newEnemy setDirection:DirUp];
        newEnemy.position = [MainScene getPositionForGridCoord:ccp(5,9)];
        [self spawnNewEnemy:newEnemy];
    }
    else
    {
        [self spawnNewEnemy:[self getRandomEnemy]];
    }
}
```

Alright! With this in place, we should have a pretty solid tutorial, but it's still kind of clunky, and we can definitely use some polish (coincidentally, that's the chapter we're in). So, let's continue to make it the best tutorial that it can be.

Removing the previous phases' text

Right now, the old text is just piling up, so let's clear that up. In the removePreviousTutorialPhase function, add the following block. It will grab the text, rename it (so that there are no naming conflicts by accident), quickly fade out the text, and remove it:

```
- (void) removePreviousTutorialPhase
{
    CCLabelBMFont *lblInstructions = (CCLabelBMFont*)[self
        getChildByName:@"tutorialText" recursively:NO];
```

```
lblInstructions.name = @"old_instructions";

id fadeRemoveInstructions = [CCActionSequence
  actions:[CCActionEaseInOut actionWithAction:[CCActionFadeTo
  actionWithDuration:0.5f opacity:0] rate:2], [CCActionCallBlock
  actionWithBlock:^{
  [self removeChild:lblInstructions];
}], nil];

[lblInstructions runAction:fadeRemoveInstructions];
}
```

There we go! But it still needs more polish. Let's add some graphical elements to our tutorial to better explain what we want the user to do.

Fingers pointing the way

Text is great, but what about those who can't read English? Or what about those who don't understand what we mean by **Drag Friendly Units**? It's best to have an image to show what we mean. In this case, we're going to use a small hand with the index finger pointing to show a drag motion in the intended direction.

Here's what we're going to add. Notice the finger (which is being moved to the right and fading at the same time), as well as the text above it, which we added in the previous section, as shown in this screenshot:

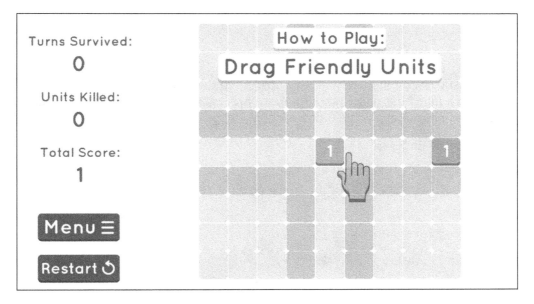

In our `showTutorialInstructions` method, we want to create a finger that will guide the user in the right direction. So, at the bottom of your `showTutorialInstructions` method, add the following block of code to create a finger and position it so that it points to the center of the middle square:

```
CCSprite *finger = [CCSprite spriteWithSpriteFrame:[[CCSpriteFrameCac
he sharedSpriteFrameCache]
    spriteFrameByName:@"imgFinger.png"]];
finger.anchorPoint = ccp(0.4,1);
finger.position = [MainScene getPositionForGridCoord:ccp(5,5)];
finger.name = @"finger";
finger.opacity = 0;
[self addChild:finger z:2];
```

Notice how we've named the finger and positioned it at z:2 (for consistency with the rest of our tutorial).

The next step is to animate our finger in the direction in which we want our users to slide their units. So, right after you've added the finger to the scene, make a call to the following function:

```
...
    [self addChild:finger z:2];

    [self runFingerArrowActionsWithFinger:finger];
}

- (void) runFingerArrowActionsWithFinger:(CCSprite*)finger
{
}
```

Here, we just passed the finger variable directly to the function (as searching for a child with a matching name takes up more processing time). Now, all we need to do with our finger image is the following:

1. Fade the finger in

2. Slide it to the right

3. Fade it out while it is sliding to the right

4. Wait a bit

5. Reposition the finger

6. Repeat

This seems fairly simple, right? It is, except when we want to sequence all of these events. In that case, the code looks fairly convoluted. This is what we want the function to look like:

```
-(void)runFingerArrowActionsWithFinger:(CCSprite*)finger
{
  Unit *u = [Unit friendlyUnit];
  if (self.tutorialPhase == 1 || self.tutorialPhase == 3)
  {
    id slideRight = [CCActionSequence actions:[CCActionEaseIn
      actionWithAction:[CCActionFadeIn actionWithDuration:0.25f]
      rate:2], [CCActionEaseInOut actionWithAction:[CCActionMoveBy
      actionWithDuration:1.0f position:ccp(u.gridWidth*2, 0)]
      rate:2],[CCActionDelay actionWithDuration:0.5f], nil];

    id fadeOutAndReposition = [CCActionSequence
      actions:[CCActionDelay actionWithDuration:0.25f],
      [CCActionEaseInOut actionWithAction:[CCActionFadeOut
      actionWithDuration:1.0f] rate:2], [CCActionDelay
      actionWithDuration:0.5f], [CCActionCallBlock
      actionWithBlock:^{
      finger.position = [MainScene
        getPositionForGridCoord:ccp(5,5)];
    }], nil];

    [finger runAction:[CCActionRepeatForever
      actionWithAction:slideRight]];
    [finger runAction:[CCActionRepeatForever
      actionWithAction:fadeOutAndReposition]];


  }
  else if (self.tutorialPhase == 2)
  {

    finger.position = [MainScene
      getPositionForGridCoord:ccp(6,5)];
    id slideLeft = [CCActionSequence actions:[CCActionEaseIn
      actionWithAction:[CCActionFadeIn actionWithDuration:0.25f]
      rate:2], [CCActionEaseInOut actionWithAction:[CCActionMoveBy
      actionWithDuration:1.0f position:ccp(-u.gridWidth*2, 0)]
      rate:2],[CCActionDelay actionWithDuration:0.5f], nil];
```

```
    id fadeOutAndReposition = [CCActionSequence
      actions:[CCActionDelay actionWithDuration:0.25f],
      [CCActionEaseInOut actionWithAction:[CCActionFadeOut
      actionWithDuration:1.0f] rate:2], [CCActionDelay
      actionWithDuration:0.5f], [CCActionCallBlock
      actionWithBlock:^{
      finger.position = [MainScene
        getPositionForGridCoord:ccp(6,5)];
    }], nil];

    [finger runAction:[CCActionRepeatForever
      actionWithAction:slideLeft]];
    [finger runAction:[CCActionRepeatForever
      actionWithAction:fadeOutAndReposition]];


  }
}
```

Essentially, the finger is going to fade in, slide to the right (while it's fading out), then get repositioned, and repeat these actions indefinitely in phase 1 and phase 3 of the tutorial (the opposite direction for phase 2).

Sadly, we're not done with coding for the entirety of the finger. We must still remove it once we wish to advance to the next phase, remember?

Therefore, in removePreviousTutorialPhase, we're just going to add a very similar removal style to the label, the only difference being that we'll apply it to the finger (and this time, we need to use the search function of getChildByName, as this function gets called at an undetermined time):

```
CCSprite *finger = (CCSprite*)[self getChildByName:@"finger"
  recursively:NO];
finger.name = @"old_finger";
id fadeRemoveFinger = [CCActionSequence actions:[CCActionEaseInOut
  actionWithAction:[CCActionFadeTo actionWithDuration:0.5f
  opacity:0] rate:2], [CCActionCallBlock actionWithBlock:^{
  [self removeChild:finger];
}], nil];
[finger runAction:fadeRemoveFinger];
```

And that's it for the finger! We've got ourselves a finger sliding in the direction we want, including a nice fade in/out. We also have the text displaying and getting removed, advancing text, and so on. The only thing left to do is to make sure our users are allowed to move their units only in the direction we want them to.

Rejecting non-tutorial movement

Our tutorial works as intended only when they move in a specific order. So, we need to restrict their initial movements when going through the tutorial.

In `Unit.m`, in the `touchMoved` function, we want to make sure that the unit can only begin to be dragged when they're going in the correct direction in the first three phases. So add the following if statement to the `touchMoved` function (when the distance is less than `20`):

```
if (!self.isBeingDragged && ccpDistance(touchPos,
  self.touchDownPos) >20)
{
  ...

    if (
  (((MainScene*)self.parent).tutorialPhase == 1 &&
    self.dragDirection != DirRight) ||
  (((MainScene*)self.parent).tutorialPhase == 2 &&
    (self.dragDirection != DirLeft || self.unitValue == 1)) ||
  (((MainScene*)self.parent).tutorialPhase == 3 &&
    self.dragDirection != DirRight))
    {
      self.isBeingDragged = NO;
      self.dragDirection = DirStanding;
    }
}
```

This is why we created the `tutorialPhase` object as a property—so that we can access the phase from within another class. But what's going on here is essentially a check of the tutorial phase, and if it's any one of phase 1, 2, or 3, it does another check to see whether `dragDirection` is indicating the correct way. There's a second check that's done for phase 2, as it's not allowed to be the unit with a value of 1.

If any of this comes out to true, we set `isBeingDragged` to `NO` and the drag direction to standing (so that no unexpected behavior happens in phase 2).

That's it for the tutorial! It took a while, but it's not only simple and quick; it's also fairly comprehensive, while not affecting the experience of the game.

Then, once our tutorial ends, it seamlessly flows into a regular game from that point. The other advantage is as follows: suppose players lose, don't finish, or hit menu or restart; or the phone dies at some point during the tutorial. When they come back, the tutorial will simply start from the beginning, which is good and intentional.

The key takeaway from the tutorial is to keep it short, save when they've completed it, and test all possible "dumb" ways a user could try to mess up the tutorial (hence the last part, about rejecting wrong movements).

Sharing on Facebook and Twitter (and more)

Sharing games on social media is very common these days. Our game will not be an exception to that. It's not only an effective marketing tool for your game, as users promote the game for you on their social media pages, but also a great way for engagement to rise, as humans love competition. Being able to share and compare their scores (and indirectly compete) makes users want to play the game even more, which makes it a win-win situation for both the developers and players.

Using the built-in share feature

The easiest way to integrate Facebook, Twitter, messaging, e-mail, and other sharing options is through the UIActivityView object. It's the same sharing you'll see when you press the button in the bottom-left corner of the photos app.

Basically, all we need to do is tell the ActivityView object what we want to display and what activity types we want to exclude, and then present the view controller over the CCDelegate.

First, we need to create the **Share** button.

Creating the Share button

In GameOverScene.m, add the following block of code to the initWithScoreData method. This will create a **Share** button at the bottom center of our game over screen:

```
//add share buttons
CCButton *btnShare = [CCButton buttonWithTitle:@""
  spriteFrame:[[CCSpriteFrameCache sharedSpriteFrameCache]
  spriteFrameByName:@"btnShare.png"]];

[btnShare setTarget:self selector:@selector(openShareView)];
btnShare.position = ccp(winSize.width/2, winSize.height * 0.1);
[self addChild:btnShare];
```

Then, create the method that the share button will call when it is pressed (this must be added now, or else the game will crash when you reach `GameOverScene`):

```
- (void) openShareView
{

}
```

Run the game, and when you get to the game over screen, you'll see the share button in the bottom center. Right now, it doesn't do anything, so let's display the activity view.

Creating a variable for the current score

We need a way to track the player's current score and the score of the most recent play. Even though we can pass that information to the game over scene, unless we store that value in an instance variable, we won't be able to use it in our sharing.

So, in `GameOverScene.h`, add a variable for the current score, like this:

```
@interface GameOverScene : CCScene <CCTableViewDataSource>
{
    CGSize winSize;
    NSArray *arrScores;
    NSInteger highScoreIndex;

    //add this:
    NSInteger numCurrentScore;
}
```

Then, in the `initWithScoreData` method, we add the following line so that we can grab the total score that was passed to the scene:

```
numCurrentScore = [dict[DictTotalScore] integerValue];
```

Now we're ready to actually use the score in the text that we share.

Creating the UIActivityView object

In the `openShareView` method you just created, add these few lines of code (explanation afterwards):

```
NSString *textToShare = [NSString stringWithFormat:@"I scored %d
    in MathGame! See if you can beat me!",numCurrentScore];
```

```
NSString *appID = @"123456789"; //change to YOUR app's ID
NSURL *appStoreURL = [NSURL URLWithString:[NSString
  stringWithFormat:@"https://itunes.apple.com/app/id%@", appID]];

NSArray *objectsToShare = @[textToShare, appStoreURL];

UIActivityViewController *activityVC = [[UIActivityViewController
  alloc] initWithActivityItems:objectsToShare
  applicationActivities:nil];
```

First comes the text that we're going to display. We need to keep it short for a few reasons. The most important reason is that Twitter allows only 140 characters, so we need to make sure we don't cross that. The second reason is that our potential future players might not read it if it's longer than a sentence or two. Finally, we want the *generic message* that's going to be sent to at least feel personal. It has to be like reading a conversation between two best friends.

Next is the link to the App Store, which also takes in the app's ID. Notice the appID variable is just 1 through 9. This isn't the exact app ID at the moment (not even for the book's project), so what we're going to do is modify this line of code when we create the app in iTunes Connect (or if you already have an app created, you can use that app ID now).

After that is the array of objects to be included in the share. Simply add them to an array.

Finally, we create the UIActivityViewController object with the objectsToShare array.

But it's not yet displaying anything, so let's handle that.

Displaying UIActivityViewController

After you've initialized the activityVC variable in the openShareView method, add the following block of code. It will ensure that the activity view doesn't show certain activities, and then present the view controller over the shared CCDelegate:

```
NSArray *excludeActivities = @[UIActivityTypeAirDrop,
    UIActivityTypePrint,
    UIActivityTypeAssignToContact,
    UIActivityTypeSaveToCameraRoll,
    UIActivityTypeAddToReadingList,
    UIActivityTypePostToFlickr,
```

```
    UIActivityTypePostToVimeo];

  activityVC.excludedActivityTypes = excludeActivities;

  [[CCDirector sharedDirector] presentViewController:activityVC
    animated:YES completion:nil];
```

Since we don't want the user to print anything, assign anything to a contact, or add it to their reading list (Flickr, Vimeo, and so on), we need to exclude these activities, which basically means they won't show up on the view that appears when the user taps the share button.

This is a list of all the possible `UIAcitivityTypes`:

- `UIActivityTypeAddToReadingList;`
- `UIActivityTypeAirDrop;`
- `UIActivityTypeAssignToContact;`
- `UIActivityTypeCopyToPasteboard;`
- `UIActivityTypeMail;`
- `UIActivityTypeMessage;`
- `UIActivityTypePostToFacebook;`
- `UIActivityTypePostToFlickr;`
- `UIActivityTypePostToTencentWeibo;`
- `UIActivityTypePostToTwitter;`
- `UIActivityTypePostToVimeo;`
- `UIActivityTypePostToWeibo;`
- `UIActivityTypePrint;`
- `UIActivityTypeSaveToCameraRoll;`

So, for your own projects, feel free to include or exclude as many or as few of these as you wish. For example, if you're sharing a video, you can very easily allow Vimeo or saving the photos.

That's it! If you run the game at this point and click on the **Share** button, you'll see the activity view pop up, along with the various buttons for messaging, e-mail, Facebook, and Twitter. Clicking on any of these will load the respective view, along with the message and URL that was added.

When adding this to your own project, the key thing to note is the exclusion list.

Here's what the final version looks like:

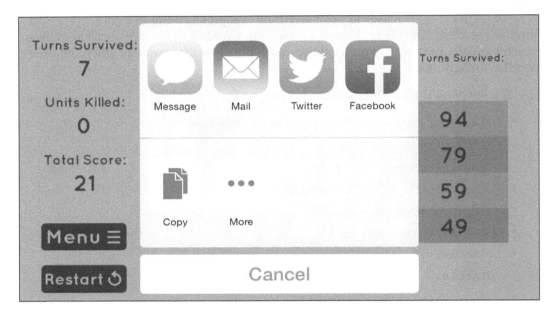

Adding a screenshot to the share

Even though we're adding some text and including a link to the game on the App Store, we should probably also include a screenshot because it's more likely someone will at least check out the game if there's a screenshot attached.

That being said, we don't really want a screenshot from the game over screen, so we'll have to grab a screenshot of the game right before we transition to GameOverScene.

So, open up MainScene.m and add the following method. It will take a screenshot of the game:

```
-(UIImage*)screenshot
{
    [CCDirector sharedDirector].nextDeltaTimeZero = YES;
```

```
CCRenderTexture* rtx =
[CCRenderTexture renderTextureWithWidth:winSize.width
  height:winSize.height];
[rtx begin];
  [[[CCDirector sharedDirector] runningScene] visit];
[rtx end];

return [rtx getUIImage];
}
```

Then, in the endGame method, let's call the preceding method and store it in a local variable so that we can pass it to the GameOverScene data:

```
UIImage *image = [self takeScreenshot];

NSDictionary *scoreData = @{DictTotalScore : @(numTotalScore),
    DictTurnsSurvived :@(numTurnSurvived),
    DictUnitsKilled :@(numUnitsKilled),
    DictHighScoreIndex :@(hsIndex),
    @"screenshot" : image};
```

Notice the addition of the @"screenshot" key to the scoreData dictionary. This will pass our UIImage so that we can grab it in GameOverScene.

Next, in GameOverScene.h, add a variable for the screenshot, like this:

```
@interface GameOverScene : CCScene <CCTableViewDataSource>
{
  CGSize winSize;
  NSArray *arrScores;
  NSInteger highScoreIndex;
  NSInteger numCurrentScore;

  //add this:
  UIImage *screenshot;
}
```

Then in our initWithScoreData method in GameOverScene.m, we want to store the screenshot in the variable from the dictionary using the @"screenshot" key:

```
screenshot = dict[@"screenshot"];
```

Finally, in our `openShareView` method of the game over scene, all we need to do is add the screenshot variable to the `objectsToShare` array, and it will be automatically included:

```
NSArray *objectsToShare = @[textToShare, myWebsite, screenshot];
```

And that's it! By running the game now and getting to the share button, you'll see the image, whether you share via Facebook, Twitter, messages, or e-mail.

If you really want to get fancy, you can allow users to save the image just in case they want to keep it for their own records. To do that, just remove the `SaveToCameraRoll` option from the exclusion array in the `openShareView` method.

Here's what your game looks like with the screenshot added (sharing via Facebook):

Turning sounds on and off

Right now, we have sound effects and music playing all the time no matter what. Even though you might be someone who enjoys listening to sounds or music, when you design your games (as it's definitely an element that increases user engagement), you would want to be open to the fact that people just don't like to hear any sound at times. Thus, we must give them the option to turn the sound on and off.

No options or settings? Main menu it is!

Since we don't have a pause screen, options, settings, or anything similar, we're going to add the buttons to turn the sound on and off to the main menu. This means that a lot less code is required to add the buttons, instead of creating an entirely new scene exclusively for them. This arrangement also stays consistent with the clean feel of the game.

> If you want to make a pause screen and add these two buttons to it, then go ahead by all means. The code, however, will be slightly different from what will be described here because if you push a CCScene instead of replace (which essentially allows you to pause the game while going to a new scene temporarily), and then pop off the scene that you pushed (in other words, resume the paused game), you need to make sure that the correct variables get set to false.

Creating the buttons

First, we're going to create the sound and music on/off buttons in the main menu. These are going to be a bit different from normal buttons because instead of just a normal button press, they're going to need to swap between the on and off states.

In `MenuScene.m`, let's create the initial buttons in the `init` method:

```
if ((self=[super init]))
{

    //these values range 0 to 1.0, so use float to get ratio
    CCNode *background = [CCNodeColor nodeWithColor:[CCColor
        whiteColor]];
    [self addChild:background];

    winSize = [CCDirector sharedDirector].viewSize;
    CCButton *btnPlay = [CCButton buttonWithTitle:@""
        spriteFrame:[CCSpriteFrame frameWithImageNamed:
        @"btnPlay.png"]];
    btnPlay.position = ccp(winSize.width/2, winSize.height * 0.5);
    [btnPlay setTarget:self selector:@selector(goToGame)];
    [self addChild:btnPlay];

    //add the sound and music buttons:
```

```
CCButton *btnSound = [CCButton buttonWithTitle:@""
    spriteFrame:[[CCSpriteFrameCache sharedSpriteFrameCache]
    spriteFrameByName:@"btnSoundOn.png"]];
[btnSound setBackgroundSpriteFrame:[[CCSpriteFrameCache
    sharedSpriteFrameCache] spriteFrameByName:
    @"btnSoundOff.png"] forState:CCControlStateSelected];
btnSound.position = ccp(winSize.width * 0.35, winSize.height *
    0.2);
[btnSound setTogglesSelectedState:YES];
[btnSound setTarget:self selector:@selector(soundToggle)];
[self addChild:btnSound];

CCButton *btnMusic = [CCButton buttonWithTitle:@""
    spriteFrame:[[CCSpriteFrameCache sharedSpriteFrameCache]
    spriteFrameByName:@"btnMusicOn.png"]];
[btnMusic setBackgroundSpriteFrame:[[CCSpriteFrameCache
    sharedSpriteFrameCache] spriteFrameByName:
    @"btnMusicOff.png"] forState:CCControlStateSelected];
btnMusic.position = ccp(winSize.width * 0.65, winSize.height *
    0.2);
[btnMusic setTogglesSelectedState:YES];
[btnMusic setTarget:self selector:@selector(musicToggle)];
[self addChild:btnMusic];

    . . .
}
```

Then we need to make sure we create the methods that the buttons will be calling when they're pressed:

```
-(void)soundToggle
{

}

-(void)musicToggle
{

}
```

Running the game at this point will result in what is shown in the following screenshot. If you press either of the buttons, they will switch between each other, and if you exit and come back, the buttons will be reset to their original state.

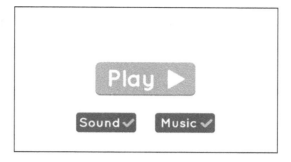

Creating the keys

What we need to do to grab (and store) the sound and music variables is make use of NSUserDefaults, just as we did in the past. To remove any user error when coding, we want to define constants for our dictionary keys.

Since MainScene has been imported into all of our classes, we can safely define the constant there. So, open MainScene.h and add the following code to the top of the file, along with the other constants:

```
FOUNDATION_EXPORT NSString *const KeySound;
FOUNDATION_EXPORT NSString *const KeyMusic;
```

Then, in MainScene.m, add this code at the top of the file with the rest of the constants so that they are defined:

```
NSString *const KeySound = @"keySound";
NSString *const KeyMusic = @"keyMusic";
```

Now we're able to grab the data that's been stored as well as efficiently save any values if we need to.

Grabbing the sound and music Boolean from NSUserDefaults

We want to store the data in a variable so that we don't have to read and write again and again from NSUserDefaults, and can do so only when we really need to.

Therefore, in MainScene.h, add two Boolean variables for sound on/off and music on/off, like this:

```
@interface MenuScene :CCNode
{
  CGSize winSize;
  BOOL isSoundOn, isMusicOn;
}
```

Then, after you've added the buttons to the scene in the init method of MainScene.m, read the sound and music values from NSUserDefaults using the keys you just defined:

```
isSoundOn = [[NSUserDefaults standardUserDefaults]
  boolForKey:KeySound];
isMusicOn = [[NSUserDefaults standardUserDefaults]
  boolForKey:KeyMusic];
```

Now we want to actually tell the sound and music buttons whether or not they should show their **X** mark or check mark. To do so, we'll just set the selected value to whatever the opposite of the variable is. That's because if the sound is not on, we want to show the selected version:

```
btnSound.selected= !isSoundOn;
btnMusic.selected= !isMusicOn;
```

This works, but there's no way to test it, so let's actually modify the values when the respective buttons are pressed.

Setting and saving the values

In the soundToggle method, we're going to set the isSoundOn variable to the opposite of itself (toggle it on and off). Right after that, we're going to set (and save) its value to the key we defined earlier:

```
- (void)soundToggle
{
  isSoundOn = !isSoundOn;
```

```
    [[NSUserDefaults standardUserDefaults] setBool:isSoundOn
      forKey:KeySound];
    [[NSUserDefaults standardUserDefaults] synchronize];
}
```

Then we're going to do the same for the `isMusicOn` variable in the `musicToggle` method:

```
- (void)musicToggle
{
    isMusicOn = !isMusicOn;
    [[NSUserDefaults standardUserDefaults] setBool:isMusicOn
      forKey:KeyMusic];
    [[NSUserDefaults standardUserDefaults] synchronize];
}
```

If you run the game now, you'll be able to switch between the true/false variables of the sound and music, and when you either go to another scene and come back, or exit the game and come back, the values will be retained from whatever you last set them to. But it's still not pausing the music or turning off the sound, so let's fix that.

Pausing/resuming background music and sound

If the background music is playing when the music button is pressed, we'll need to pause it, and vice versa for when it's not playing.

To start, let's go to the `musicToggle` method and add a check for the `isMusicOn` variable. If it is enabled, we can play the background music. Otherwise, we'll just pause the music until the user turns it on again:

```
isMusicOn ? [[OALSimpleAudio sharedInstance] playBg] :
    [[OALSimpleAudio sharedInstance] bgPaused];
```

After that, we'll also add a check to see whether the `isSoundOn` is enabled. If it is, we'll play the `buttonClick` sound effect:

```
if (isSoundOn)
[[OALSimpleAudio sharedInstance] playEffect:@"buttonClick.mp3"];
```

We're going to do the same for the `toggleSound` method as well as the `goToGame` method, both of which are methods that get called when a button is pressed. Therefore, we are going to play a button click sound effect (only if the sound is enabled):

```
- (void)goToGame
{
  if (isSoundOn)
    [[OALSimpleAudio sharedInstance]
      playEffect:@"buttonClick.mp3"];
  [[CCDirector sharedDirector] replaceScene:[MainScene scene]];
}

- (void)soundToggle
{
    ...

  if (isSoundOn)
    [[OALSimpleAudio sharedInstance]
      playEffect:@"buttonClick.mp3"];
}
```

For `MenuScene`, all is done! If you press the music button and/or the sound button, you'll notice the effects turning on and off, just as intended. Now that we have handled `MenuScene`, let's go for every other location where we'll be playing the sound effects (and starting the music).

Alternatively, you can create a class that has methods for starting and stopping the background music, playing certain sound effects, and playing the button click, all using `OALSimpleAudio`.

Then you can locate and replace all the instances of `OALSimpleAudio` with your own custom class.

Handling MainScene sound

Since we have sound effects and music playing in just about every class of this game, we need to make sure they play only when the corresponding value is true.

So for starters, let's open `MainScene.h` and add a similar variable for a sound:

```
@interface MainScene :CCScene
{
   BOOL isSoundOn;
}
```

Next, in the `init` method, make sure you grab the values from `NSUserDefaults`:

 Also make sure you set the `isSoundOn` variable in the `init` method before you attempt to play any sound effect. If you assign the value afterwards, you may experience unintended results.

```
-(id)init
{
    if ((self=[super init]))
    {
       //used for positioning items on screen
       winSize = [[CCDirector sharedDirector] viewSize];
    isSoundOn = [[NSUserDefaults standardUserDefaults]
       boolForKey:KeySound];

       . . .
    }
    return self;
    return self;
    }
```

In `MainScene.m`, search for `OALSimpleAudio`, and go to every instance of it, adding the following `if` statement above it so that the sound effect plays only when that particular sound is enabled:

```
if (isSoundOn)
    . . .
```

There should be two in `playUnitCombineSound`, one in `goToMenu`, one in `restartGame`, and one in `moveUnit`. Obviously, if you have more sound effects playing, then you should add them there as well, but these are the five that are present at this point.

Repeating for GameOverScene (and any other scenes)

It's basically the same as `MainScene`, so there won't be too much explanation. But all you really need to do is the following:

- Create the `isSoundOn` variable in `GameOverScene.h`
- Assign the value in the `init` method from `NSUserDefaults`
- Add the if statement before every sound effect that gets played
- Since this is your only other scene, move on to `AppDelegate`

Handling AppDelegate music

We need to make sure the music doesn't randomly start playing when users first load the game if they had decided to turn it off in a previous version.

So in `AppDelegate.m`, add the following if statement before the call to the `playBgWithLoop` method. Note that we don't need to store it in a variable because we're going to use it only once:

```
if ([[NSUserDefaults standardUserDefaults] boolForKey:KeyMusic])
    [[OALSimpleAudiosharedInstance] playBgWithLoop:YES];
```

Making sure that sound/music starts enabled

One of the things we want to make sure of is that the sound and music start as enabled when the user starts the game. By default, any Boolean in `NSUserDefaults` is false. Therefore, we need to make sure that both get set to true before the game starts, but only on the first time they run the game.

So in `AppDelegate.m`, at the very beginning of `startScene`, let's add code to check whether they've played before:

```
- (CCScene*) startScene
{
    //if they have not played before (in other words, first time
      playing)
    if (![[NSUserDefaults standardUserDefaults]
      boolForKey:@"hasPlayedBefore"])
    {
```

```
    [[NSUserDefaults standardUserDefaults] setBool:YES
        forKey:KeySound];
    [[NSUserDefaults standardUserDefaults] setBool:YES
        forKey:KeyMusic];
    [[NSUserDefaults standardUserDefaults] setBool:YES
        forKey:@"hasPlayedBefore"];

    [[NSUserDefaults standardUserDefaults] synchronize];
}


...


    return [MainScene scene];//[CCBReader loadAsScene:@"MainScene"];
}
```

And that's it! It took a little bit of careful planning to make sure we handled every case that the user could run into, but that's the entire point of polishing your game—making sure that no matter what your user does or can do, the game responds appropriately and as intended.

The key takeaways from adding on/off settings for sound and music are as follows: storing the value in the NSUserDefaults, grabbing that value from a local variable in each scene, and using that variable to determine whether you should play a sound effect or not. If you want to be sure you've gotten all the instances, look up the project for OALSimpleAudio and go through all the classes you've created.

Make sure that you check for the variable for any future sound effects you add.

Game Center leaderboards

We've already got a set of top 20 high scores that are stored on the user's device, so why not make a global leaderboard? In fact, even though many players don't use Game Center when they play games, it is yet another element that drives engagement. Plus (and this is the really cool part)—if you didn't know already—you can actually have players rate your game within Game Center. It's not even an extra feature or anything, as they can just tap the star count at the top of the leaderboard or achievement pane and it'll send the rating to the App Store.

Creating a leaderboard to display in our game isn't just about code, so we have to create the leaderboard in iTunes Connect first. Before we can create the app in iTunes Connect, we need to set up an App ID.

Creating the App ID

At this point, if you wish to add a leaderboard, you must sign up for an Apple developer account if you don't have one already. In *Chapter 1, Refreshing Our Cocos2d Knowledge,* the signup process was explained. Otherwise, if you're just following along for practice, feel free to do so, but you cannot create leaderboards or achievements without a developer account.

First, you need to create the App ID from the developer website. Go to `https://developer.apple.com/devcenter/ios/index.action` and log in to your Apple account that has the iOS developer license on it.

Once logged in, under **iOS Dev Center**, go to the **Certificates, Identifiers & Profiles** section, as shown in this screenshot:

From here, go to the **Identifiers** section so that we can create an App ID, as shown in the following screenshot:

Then begin to create an App ID by clicking on the **+** button in the top-right corner. Here, we need to enter a name for the App ID, the name of the bundle identifier (which is generally reverse DNS notation; for example, `www.keitgames.com` might have `com.keitgames.mygame` as the bundle ID), as well as any services we want (which we'll leave as the default for now). This is shown in the following screenshot for your reference:

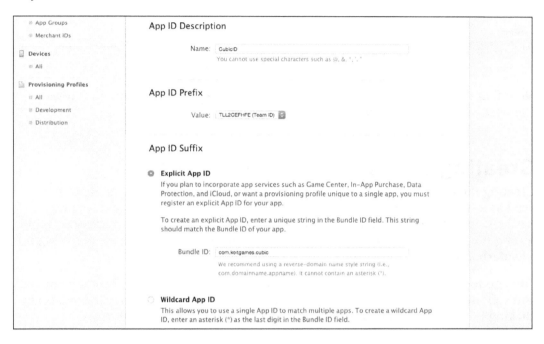

Make sure you use your own bundle identifier (the preceding screenshot simply shows an example and where it all goes).

Once that's done, click on **Continue** and then on **Submit**. Then the App ID should be created.

Next, in the Xcode project's settings, select the iOS target and update the bundle identifier to the one you just created.

Now that the bundle ID and App ID are set up, we can create the app in iTunes Connect, and it will allow us to set up and test our leaderboards.

Creating the app in iTunes Connect

Creating the app in iTunes Connect is relatively simple, and is only going to be used as a wireframe so that we can create the leaderboards. In the next chapter, we'll cover all the details; for now you just need to know that the only reason we're setting it up in iTunes Connect now (instead of later) is for the purpose of setting up a leaderboard.

First, go to `https://itunesconnect.apple.com/WebObjects/iTunesConnect.woa` and sign in to your developer account. Then click on **My Apps**, create a new app by clicking on the **+** button in the top-left corner, and click on **New iOS App**.

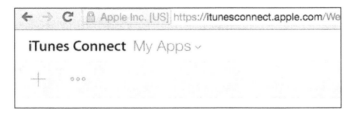

Then fill in the information it asks, including the App ID you created earlier. The SKU doesn't really matter, as it's for your own internal use.

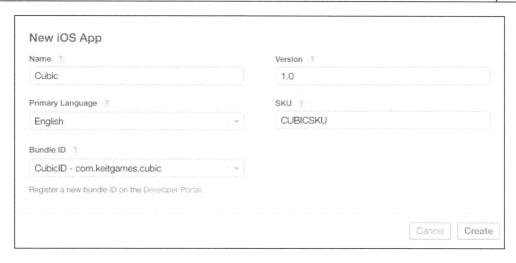

Once the app has been created in iTunes connect, click on **Game Center**.

When it asks whether it's for a single game or multiple games, that's up to you to decide when creating projects on your own. But for the purpose of this book's project, we're going to create it for a single game.

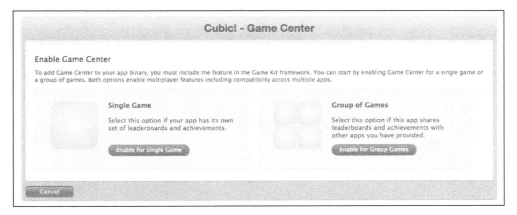

After that, you'll be taken to the Game Center setup screen, and you're ready to move on to the next step.

Creating the leaderboard

From the Game Center setup section within iTunes Connect, click on the **Add Leaderboard** button and then on **Single Leaderboard**.

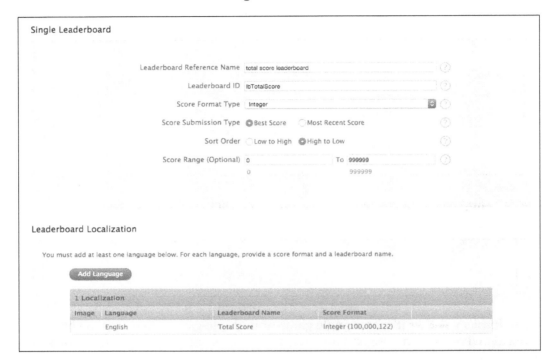

The leaderboard reference is for internal use within iTunes Connect, just in case you wish to search for it (or know at a glance which leaderboard it is). The **Leaderboard ID** will be used within the code, so it should be something unique and distinct from your other leaderboards (if you've created any). The score format is only whole numbers, so we'll use the **Integer** format. We want only the best score to be submitted (as only one score per person can exist in a leaderboard) and sorted from High to Low. Finally, we want the range to be from 0 to 999,999. Technically, we don't have to set this, but we're going to anyway.

Next, we add a language. Here's an example showing **English**:

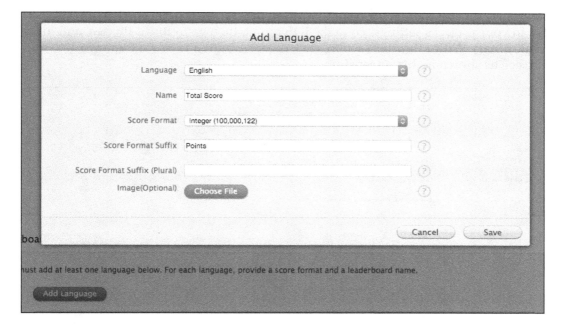

The **Name** is the title at the top of the leaderboard that the users will see, so we want it to be obvious which leaderboard it is. The **Score Format** is the same as what you just saw. The **Score Format Suffix** works as follow: since we have **Points**, a score of 625 will look like **625 Points** in the leaderboard. If you think it would look weird to include the word **Points** in every score, feel free to leave it out, but for now, we're going to have it in there.

Once all of this information has been entered, click on **Save** at the bottom. And voilà! It's created! What comes next is coding the Game Center login, authentication, leaderboard presentation, submitting the score, and everything else that comes with handling Game Center.

Adding the GameKit framework

Before we do any coding, we need to include the GameKit framework in our project. So, in your project's settings, go to the **iOS target**, then go to **Build Phases**, and in the **Link Binary With Libraries** section, click on the **+** button to add a framework to the project, as shown in this screenshot:

Then, search for `gamekit` (case insensitive), click on the `GameKit.framework` result, and then click on **Add**.

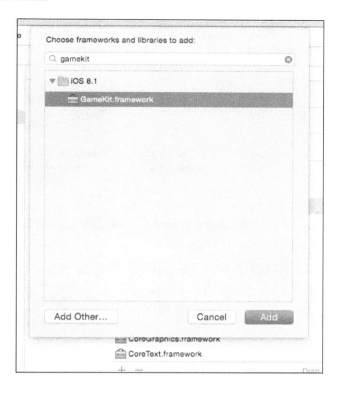

And we're done! Now we're ready to code.

GameKit helper files

For the sake of simplicity, you can just copy the `GKHelper` files to your project (make sure you have the **Copy** checkbox selected). It's not that coding the Game Center stuff is hard — it's the same for literally every project that has Game Center. So why waste time manually typing the code when you can just have the files ready?

Essentially, what the `GKHelper` singleton class does is manage your `GKLocalPlayer` (the currently logged-in user in Game Center on the device), any calls to and from the server, and any leaderboard score posting and achievement tracking.

The GKHelper class was created using the online tutorial
http://www.raywenderlich.com/23189/whats-new-with-game-center-in-ios-6, if you're looking for more explanation. There is another guide at http://www.appcoda.com/ios-game-kit-framework/ that covers Game Center in depth. Refer to it if you're getting stuck, or still need extra help (as it can be confusing for those new to coding Game Center).

This is important: Suppose you're getting this error message:

```
GameKitHelper ERROR: {
NSLocalizedDescription = "The requested operation could not be
  completed because this application is not recognized by Game
  Center.";
}
```

Then you must go to device **Settings | Game Center** and enable **Sandbox**, as shown in this screenshot:

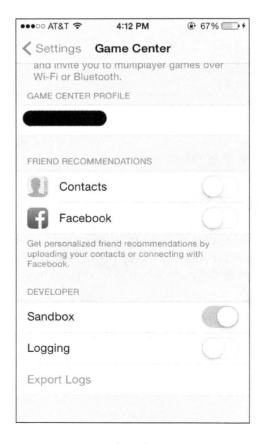

Authenticating the user

Now that everything is in place, created, and ready for use, we can begin to code the actual leaderboard and make it appear when users sign in to Game Center.

First, we need to authenticate the local player; that is, have them sign in if they aren't signed in already, or just send a request for the GKLocalPlayer.

We're going to do this at the beginning of our app, so in AppDelegate.m, import the GKHelper.h file and add the following method call to the top of the startScene method:

```
[[GKHelper sharedGameKitHelper] authenticateLocalPlayer];
```

If everything was done correctly, when you run the game at this point, you should see a banner going across the top of your screen welcoming the currently logged-in player. If not, it will ask them to log in.

If you're getting an error message that says something along the lines of a requested operation being cancelled or disabled, go to the **Settings** app and then to **Game Center**. Try either logging in and out again, or enabling the **Sandbox** mode at the bottom (see the preceding screenshot). This should fix it.

Creating the Game Center button

We want a button for access to the leaderboards and other Game Center stuff, so in the **GameOverScene.m** file's init method, add the following code. It will create a button in the bottom-right corner of the screen:

```
//add Game Center buttons
CCButton *btnGameCenter = [CCButton buttonWithTitle:@"" spriteFrame:[[
CCSpriteFrameCache sharedSpriteFrameCache] spriteFrameByName:@"btnGame
Center.png"]];

[btnGameCenter setTarget:self selector:@selector(viewGameCenter1)];
btnGameCenter.position = ccp(0.75, 0.1);
btnGameCenter.positionType = CCPositionTypeNormalized;
[self addChild:btnGameCenter];
```

We also want to display the leaderboards, and this requires the GKHelper, so at the top of GameOverScene.m, import the GKHelper.h file:

```
#import "GKHelper.h"
```

Then create the `viewGameCenter` method, which is simply a call for presenting the leaderboards:

```
- (void) viewGameCenter
{
    [[GKHelper sharedGameKitHelper] presentLeaderboards];
}
```

If you run the game at this point and get to the game over scene, you'll see a button for **Game Center** in the bottom-right corner, and when clicked on (and if you're signed in to Game Center), it'll open the leaderboard. The only thing left to do now is to submit the score to Game Center so it can be seen in the leaderboard.

Submitting the score

Since our `GKHelper` class can do all of the score reporting for us, all we need to do is call the respective function. Since we know `GameOverScene` will contain the total score from the most recent game, we can use the passed-in dictionary as the score value we submit to the leaderboard.

So, in the `init` method of `GameOverScene.m`, add a call to the `submitScore` function:

```
[[GKHelper sharedGameKitHelper] submitScore:[dict[DictTotalScore]
integerValue]];
```

And that's it! It took a while to set up, and about 10 lines of code, but we have a global leaderboard.

There are two things to note here:

- You may want to implement achievements, but that code has not been implemented in the `GKHelper` class yet, so unfortunately, you're on your own. Although this is not too difficult, it wasn't necessary for this game, so it was skipped. As linked earlier, there's a great resource at `http://www.appcoda.com/ios-game-kit-framework/` that explains how to implement achievements. It was written in March 2014, so the code should still work by the time you read this book.

- While implementing leaderboards, if you ever run into an issue, make sure that everything, from the iTunes Connect setup to the Game Center to **Sandbox** mode and the code itself, is all in line. Game Center can be tricky and annoying. It's gotten better over the years, but can still be a bit finicky. If you're still having issues, it's likely that you're not the only one. A great place to start searching is Stack Overflow. If you aren't familiar with the site, don't worry. They have a question-and-answer format where tons of people have asked questions about code and other issues, and many more have given correct answers.

And that's it for Game Center! The last thing to do to polish our project includes creating a custom transition between scenes to make the game feel more robust, instead of just instantly shifting back and forth between scenes.

Slide transition

Although it's fine for testing purposes, instant transitions between our scenes (as well as the game suddenly showing up when it first loads) are bad. We're going to add a nice quick slide between each scene. In other words, when the user taps a button or an event happens that's supposed to replace the scene with a new scene, we're going to make it seem as if all the scenes are on one giant white sheet, just out of view of the user.

Creating a generic slide function

Since we're going to be doing this all over the place, we need a function that's generic enough for us to pass to it any scene from any location, and it will do exactly what we want it to do.

So again, since `MainScene.h` is imported everywhere, we're going to create our generic function in it. Open `MainScene.h` and add this enumeration above the @ interface line:

```
NS_ENUM(NSInteger, kMoveDirection)
{
  kMoveDirectionUp,
  kMoveDirectionDown,
  kMoveDirectionLeft,
  kMoveDirectionRight
};

@interface MainScene :CCScene
{ ... }
```

This will allow us to tell the generic function in which direction to slide our scene.

After that, add the following method declaration in `MainScene.h`:

```
+(void)rubberBandToScene:(CCNode*)scene fromParent:(CCNode*)parent
    withDuration:(CGFloat)duration withDirection:
    (enumkMoveDirection)direction;
```

The parameters this method takes are the scene you want to transition to, the parent (the scene you're currently on), how long you want the slide to last, and in what direction you want the slide to occur.

Next, in `MainScene.m`, add the actual function. It will slide our scene into the view and then replace it with `CCDirector` (the detailed explanation is in the comments):

```
+(void)rubberBandToScene:(CCScene*)scene
    fromParent:(CCNode*)parent withDuration:(CGFloat)duration
    withDirection:(enumkMoveDirection)direction
{
  //grab the view size, so we know the width/height of the screen
  CGSize winSize = [[CCDirector sharedDirector] viewSize];

  //add the new scene to the current scene
  [parent addChild:scene z:-1];

  //set a distance to "over move" by
  NSInteger distance = 25;

  //variables for how much to move in each direction
  CGPoint posBack = ccp(0,0);
  CGPoint posForward = ccp(0,0);

  //determine the specifics based on which direction the slide is
  going to go
  if (direction == kMoveDirectionUp)
  {
    posBack.y = -distance;
    posForward.y = winSize.height + distance*2;
    scene.position = ccp(0,-winSize.height);
  }
  elseif (direction == kMoveDirectionDown)
  {
    posBack.y = distance;
    posForward.y = -(winSize.height + distance*2);
    scene.position = ccp(0,winSize.height);
  }
  elseif (direction == kMoveDirectionLeft)
  {
```

```
    posBack.x = distance;
    posForward.x = -(winSize.width + distance*2);
    scene.position = ccp(winSize.width, 0);
  }
  elseif (direction == kMoveDirectionRight)
  {
    posBack.x = -distance;
    posForward.x = winSize.width + distance*2;
    scene.position = ccp(-winSize.width,0);
  }

  //declare the slide actions
  id slideBack = [CCActionEaseInOut actionWithAction:[CCActionMoveBy
actionWithDuration:duration/4
  position:posBack] rate:2];
  id slideForward = [CCActionEaseInOut actionWithAction:[CCActionMoveB
y actionWithDuration:duration/2
  position:posForward] rate:2];
  id slideBackAgain = [CCActionEaseInOut actionWithAction:[CCActionMov
eBy actionWithDuration:duration/4
  position:posBack] rate:2];
  id replaceScene = [CCActionCallBlock actionWithBlock:^{

    //remove the new scene from the current scene (so we can use
  it in the replace)
    [parent removeChild:scene cleanup:NO];

    //reset its position to (0,0)
    scene.position = ccp(0,0);

    //actually replace our scene with the passed-in one
    [[CCDirector sharedDirector] replaceScene:scene];
  }];

  //arrange the actions into a sequence (which also includes the
    replacing)
  id slideSeq = [CCActionSequence actions:slideBack, slideForward,
    slideBackAgain, replaceScene, nil];

  //execute the sequence of actions
  [parent runAction:slideSeq];
}
```

However, since we're moving the scenes slightly off screen in one direction or another, we need to make sure we have enough "background" to cover the extras.

Extending the background

At the top of our `MainScene.m` files `init` method, we change our declaration of the background to the following:

```
CCNode *background = [CCNodeColor nodeWithColor:[CCColor
    whiteColor] width:winSize.width*5 height:winSize.height*5];
background.anchorPoint = ccp(0.5,0.5);
background.position = ccp(winSize.width/2, winSize.height/2);
[self addChild:background z:-2];
```

The z value is set to `-2` so that we can place the new scene at `-1` (as seen in preceding code). Thus, even though the background is five times the width and the height of the screen, the new scene will still be visible when it slides into the view.

Now the only thing left to do is to actually call the function.

Replacing the scene with a rubber band transition

Because we made such a convenient generic function, we don't need to do anything besides calling it once. So in `MainScene.m`, modify your `goToMenu` function to call the `rubberBandToScene` method you just created:

```
- (void) goToMenu
{
  if (isSoundOn)
    [[OALSimpleAudio sharedInstance]
      playEffect:@"buttonClick.mp3"];

  [MainScene rubberBandToScene:[MenuScene scene] fromParent:self
    withDuration:0.5f withDirection:kMoveDirectionDown];
}
```

Also modify the same line in the `endGame` method in `MainScene.m`:

```
- (void) endGame
{
  //right here:
  NSInteger hsIndex = [self saveHighScore];

  UIImage *image = [self takeScreenshot];
```

```
NSDictionary *scoreData = @{DictTotalScore : @(numTotalScore),
    DictTurnsSurvived :@(numTurnSurvived),
    DictUnitsKilled :@(numUnitsKilled),
    DictHighScoreIndex :@(hsIndex),
    @"screenshot" : image};

[MainScene rubberBandToScene:[GameOverScene sceneWithScoreData:
    scoreData] fromParent:self withDuration:0.5f
    withDirection:kMoveDirectionUp];

}
```

Notice that the one going to the menu is `DirectionDown`, whereas the `endGame` object is `DirectionUp`. Now run the game and press that **Menu** button. Beautiful isn't it? But that's just one of the many scene transitions we have. So let's handle the rest, shall we?

Transition in MenuScene

When we click on the **Play** button, we'd ideally want the same effect, so we first need to create the extra-large background. In `MenuScene.m`, modify the background code to look like `MainScene`:

```
-(id)init
{
  if ((self=[super init]))
  {
    winSize = [CCDirector sharedDirector].viewSize;

    //these values range 0 to 1.0, so use float to get ratio
    CCNode *background = [CCNodeColor nodeWithColor:
    [CCColorwhiteColor] width:winSize.width*5
    height:winSize.height*5];
    background.anchorPoint = ccp(0.5,0.5);
    background.position = ccp(winSize.width/2, winSize.height/2);
  [self addChild:background z:-2];
  ...
}
```

Then, in the `goToGame` function, we simply make a call to the generic function we made previously:

```
- (void)goToGame
{
  if (isSoundOn)
    [[OALSimpleAudio sharedInstance] playEffect:
      @"buttonClick.mp3"];

  [MainScene rubberBandToScene:[MainScene scene] fromParent:self
    withDuration:0.5f withDirection:kMoveDirectionUp];
}
```

Transition in GameOver

So far, we've gotten the to-menu and to-gameover transitions into the main game scene. We've also implemented the to-game transition in the main menu scene. The only thing left to do is to put the transition for to-menu and to-game in the `GameOverScene`.

To do this, you can do in `GameOverScene.m` what you've been doing so far, and modify the `replaceScene` line of code in the `goToMenu` and `restartGame` methods:

```
- (void)goToMenu
{
  //to be filled in later
  [MainScene rubberBandToScene:[MenuScene scene] fromParent:self
    withDuration:0.5f withDirection:kMoveDirectionDown];
}

- (void)restartGame
{
  //to be filled in later
  [MainScene rubberBandToScene:[MainScene scene] fromParent:self
    withDuration:0.5f withDirection:kMoveDirectionDown];
}
```

And that's it! We've managed to not only create a custom transition (compared to the rather boring transitions that Cocos2d version 3.0+ comes with) but also implement it with ease. It adds just that bit of the "Whee! This is fun!" factor, which is a good thing because it's what the players will be feeling. Happy players means higher engagement, and higher engagement means higher ratings and more referrals to their friends (which means more money in your pocket).

Other ideas for polishing

Some other ideas for polishing that weren't covered in this chapter are as follows:

- Smoother animation for characters or units
- Fluid movements (such as the Bézier effect, as covered in the previous chapter)
- No loading screen (ending the current scene looking exactly like how the next scene will begin, and transitioning instantly)
- No crashes (yes, fix all of them)
- Subtle details such as background movement or brief NPC voice-overs
- Saving the user's spot in case of an interruption (phone call, battery dead, and so on)

But these are just a few examples. There's a million little things you could do to your game to make it ever so slightly better, but alas! At some point, we need to release the game, so that's what the next chapter is going to focus on—adding the finishing touches and submitting the game to Apple.

Summary

In this chapter, you learned various ways to polish your game and really focus on some subtle, but important, elements such as on/off buttons for sound and music, sliding between scenes, and the social sharing feature.

There's always something that can be tweaked and tuned to make it more polished. For example, if you wish to learn more about more traditional sprite animations, you can do so using `CCAnimation`. There's a great reference guide for this at `http://www.cocos2d-swift.org/docs/api/Classes/CCAnimation.html`.

Notice that as of now, we still haven't come up with a name for the game. Although the name is something that all users will see and familiarize themselves with, it's not important for the development of the game, which is why it's coming last.

7
Reaching Our Destination

This chapter will be pretty light compared to the last few, as this game is ready to be finalized for release by now. We'll be going over some steps of finalization within the project, as well as stuff to do within iTunes Connect before you submit the game to be reviewed by Apple. Specifically, we'll cover the following topics in this relatively short chapter:

- Adding a default image
- Icons
- Analytics
- Preparing the App on iTunes Connect
- Releasing the game and steps after it

For this chapter, we'll be using the Chapter 7 project, as it has some bug fixes as well as some other polish elements added. It's recommended that you open this project before continuing.

At the time of writing this book, Cocos2d version 3.4 does not support native iPhone 6 or 6 Plus. So unfortunately, the art will look blurry as Apple scales up the iPhone 5 screen to match the iPhone 6 or 6 Plus resolutions. If you're determined to make native resolutions work, you can refer to a thread at http://forum.cocos2d-swift. org/t/iphone-6-ios-resolutions-and-assets/15062/68. It describes using the iPad Retina version 6 assets when running version 6 Plus, and the iPhone Retina assets when running.

Adding a default image

Now, we only need to create the launch images for every iPad and every pre-6 iPhone. Also, we're going to do a sort of hackish workaround that will make the iPhone 6 or 6 Plus graphics slightly better (though still not native), while at the same time making the iPhone 5 look better and worse at the same time (depending on how you look at it).

First, in the `Icon` folder of the project, delete the existing `Default` images, moving them to the trash rather than just removing the references.

There should be a folder called `Default Images` included in the project files, where you'll have each of the files needed for the project. Drag these files into the Xcode project (making sure you have the **Copy** checkbox checked).

Because we don't have many devices that need native default images, we're just going to skip asset catalogs for now. If you want to use them, you can, but it's not required (nor is there any real benefit) when you have the default images properly named, as we have here.

Adding the loading screen

Although the default images are the first thing the user will see, we still want a smooth transition from the initial image to our game, instead of it just suddenly changing. So, we're going to create a transition scene just for the purpose of sliding the game view into position.

First, create a new class—a subclass of `CCScene`—and call it `LoadingScene`.

Then, add the `scene` method to the `LoadingScene.h` file:

```
+(CCScene*) scene;
```

Next, replace your `LoadingScene.m` file with the following code:

```
#import "LoadingScene.h"
#import "MainScene.h"

@implementation LoadingScene
+(CCScene*) scene
{
    return [[self alloc] init];
```

```
}

-(id)init
{
  if ((self=[super init]))
  {
//sets the window size and adds a white background
    CGSize winSize = [[CCDirector sharedDirector] viewSize];
    CCNodeColor *background = [CCNodeColor nodeWithColor:[CCColor
whiteColor] width:winSize.width  height:winSize.height*5];
    background.position = ccp(0.5,0.5);
    background.positionType = CCPositionTypeNormalized;
    background.anchorPoint = ccp(0.5,0.5);
    [self addChild:background z:-2];

//creates the Cubic! Title in the middle of the screen (where it's
located in the Default.png image)
    CCLabelBMFont *lblTitle = [CCLabelBMFont labelWithString:@"Cubic!"
fntFile:@"bmTitleFont.fnt"];
    lblTitle.position = ccp(0.5,0.5);
    lblTitle.color = [CCColor colorWithRed:52/255.f green:73/255.f
blue:94/255.f];
    lblTitle.positionType = CCPositionTypeNormalized;
    [self addChild:lblTitle];

//creates a progress circle that shows the user that stuff is
happening (even though everything is technically already loaded at
this point)
    CCSprite *circle = [CCSprite spriteWithSpriteFrame:[[CCSpriteFram
eCache sharedSpriteFrameCache] spriteFrameByName:@"imgLoadingCircle.
png"]];
    CCProgressNode *loadingTime = [CCProgressNode
progressWithSprite:circle];
    loadingTime.type = CCProgressNodeTypeRadial;
    loadingTime.midpoint = ccp(0.5,0.5);
    [loadingTime runAction:[CCActionProgressFromTo
actionWithDuration:1 from:0.0f to:100.0f]];
    loadingTime.position = ccp(winSize.width/2, winSize.height * 0.2);
    [self addChild:loadingTime];

    //schedules the transition to the main menu after 2 seconds
(1 second for progress circle, and another second of waiting for a
smoother transition)
    [self scheduleOnce:@selector(transitionToMainScene) delay:2];
  }
```

```
        return self;
    }

    //method to transition using our rubber band effect created previously
    -(void)transitionToMainScene
    {
        [MainScene rubberBandToScene:[MainScene scene] fromParent:self
    withDuration:0.6 withDirection:kMoveDirectionUp];
    }

    @end
```

Understand that we want to transition to MainScene, so we have to import it.

Also notice the CCProgressNode object. This will be a ring that will simulate loading. Since our game loads relatively fast without the need for a true loading bar or other sort of progress measurement, we don't want our users getting confused when they see the same image for a few seconds on end. So, we add a CCProgressNode object that lets them know "Hey, something's happening!"

It's fairly self-explanatory when you look at the code. The midpoint is essentially like the anchor point on other CCNode objects. If you want a bar instead of a circle, just change the type. Everything else should be the same.

Switching to LoadingScene from MainScene

Finally, to make it all happen, we just need to add the import statement for LoadingScene.h to the AppDelegate.m file:

```
    #import "LoadingScene.h"
```

Then, at the bottom of your startScene method, look for the following line:

```
    return [MainScene scene];
```

Replace it with this new line of code that will go into the LoadingScene object we just created:

```
    return [LoadingScene scene];
```

If you run the game at this point, you'll see the initial default image load, then after a second or two the progress ring will appear, and finally, the loading screen will go up and off screen, and drag the `MainScene` along with it.

Now that we have handled our initial launch, let's set up the icons.

Icons

The default icon that SpriteBuilder provided us was convenient for testing but it's time we set ourselves apart and create our own icon.

 To use the template we'll be talking about in the next section, you'll need Photoshop. If you have a design team, you likely have it somewhere. If you don't have Photoshop, you can get a free trial version from its website.

Template

There are about 10 to 15 different app icon sizes, depending on which devices you plan to support and which iOS versions you're supporting. It would be a pain to manually update all of these sizes if you change your icon. Thankfully, it's easier than ever to create the required app icon sizes with a template that was created by Michael Flarup.

You can download the template from `www.appicontemplate.com`. Once it is downloaded, you can open it from Photoshop and begin using it. Once you're ready, you just have to run the action included in the download and it will generate the files for you.

There's also a very good video on how to use the template, so in the spirit of not repeating things twice, the how-to won't be shown here.

Adding the icons to the project

First, we want to get rid of the old icons, as we don't want any interference or accidental appearance on someone's device. So just delete the old icons.

Once you have your new icons created (or if you wish to use the icons included in this project), simply drag the files into Xcode, making sure that the **Copy** checkbox is checked. This is also shown in the following screenshot:

Right now, the project isn't going to use the new icons, so we need to assign the icon file to be used for each size with asset catalogs.

Asset catalog

We're going to use an asset catalog for our icons. Ideally, we should use them for our launch images as well, but since we're not supporting any crazy device sizes or orientations, it's just not necessary at the moment.

With icons, however, it's just a lot easier to create the asset catalog, then drag and drop your icons into the appropriate place based on which iOS versions you wish to support.

So first, you need to create the asset catalog in Xcode by going to the project's general settings and clicking on the **Use Asset Catalog** button.

If the asset catalog already exists, simply click on the arrow to the right of the drop-down box to navigate to that asset catalog. This is also shown in the following screenshot for your reference:

Then, with the catalog created, simply drag the images into the appropriate place based on what dimensions they need to be. The following screenshot is a rough representation of what they should be, but make sure you drag the correct images, or else Xcode will throw a warning that you're giving it an incorrectly sized image. Thankfully, the template we use gives us a good name for our images, so we can quickly see which icon is of what size.

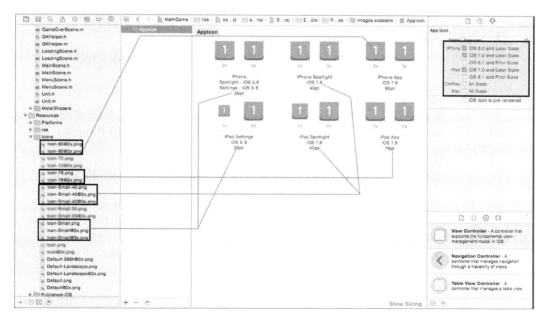

Notice that we aren't supporting **iOS 6.1 and prior** sizes. Although you may think it's just a couple of icon sizes, if you're truly willing to support iOS 6 and older versions, you must run your app on a device running an older device to make sure that nothing crashes.

Anyway, once you've added your images to the asset catalog, clean up the project, and rerun it. You'll see the **Update** icon as expected. That's it!

Analytics and user data

One final thing to do before we submit our app is to set up some quick analytics tools to determine the way our users play our game. We're going to use an API called **Flurry**. If you haven't heard of it before or you have but never used it, it's fine, as the following section will take you through the setup process.

Flurry is nice for three main reasons:

- Simplicity in setting up and using
- Detailed analytics available
- It's free! Who can argue with that?

So let's go for it, starting with the signup process.

Signing up for Flurry

Go to `http://www.flurry.com/`, and in the top-right corner, click on **Sign Up**. Fill in the information it asks for, and then click on **Sign Up**.

After that, it'll ask you which platform you wish to track analytics for. Here, since we're making an app for iPhone and iPad (a universal app for iOS), we'll select iPhone. If the app were only available on iPad, you would have selected the iPad version.

We then add the name of the app and choose which category the app falls under.

Once that's ready, click on **Create App** at the bottom, and Flurry will ask you to verify your e-mail. Once you click on the link in your e-mail (or copy the code that they send and paste it in the verification box they provide), you'll be directed to a screen letting you know that the process was a success. Then you should be given an API key.

Remember to either copy this API key somewhere or leave the web page open, as we'll need this later when we actually begin our session tracking.

After the successful setup, you should see a link to download the SDK. Download the SDK (ZIP file), and wait until it finishes. It may take a minute or so.

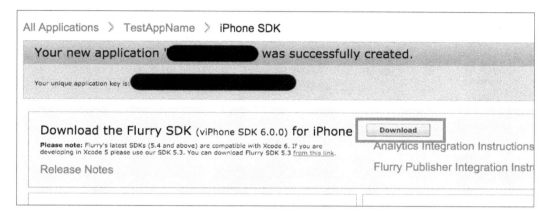

Once the SDK is downloaded and unzipped, we're ready to add Flurry to our project.

Adding Flurry to your project

Since the Flurry API should be included with all the other libraries, in the downloaded SDK, you should see a `Flurry` folder. Drag that entire folder into the `libs` folder of Xcode (making sure that the copy checkbox is checked).

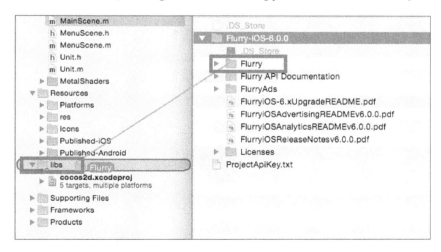

Then, we'll want to make sure that the proper frameworks are included in our project so that Flurry can do its things properly. So, in the **Build Phases** of our project, we're going to add a few frameworks. Simply click on the + button under the **Link Binary with Libraries** section.

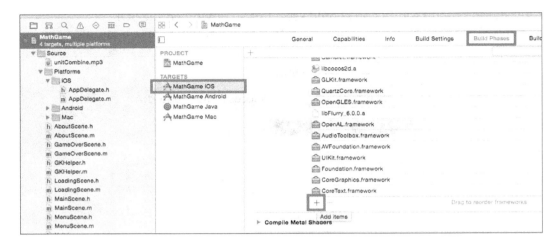

Then search for and add the following frameworks:

- `Security.framework`
- `SystemConfiguration.framework`
- `CFNetwork.framework`

Finally, the library has been included in our project, and we can import the Flurry header to our `AppDelegate.m` file, and start our tracking session in the `application:didFinishLaunchingWithOptions` method:

```
#import "Flurry.h"

@implementation AppController

- (BOOL)application:(UIApplication *)application didFinishLaunchingWit
hOptions:(NSDictionary *)launchOptions
{

    [Flurry startSession:@"API_KEY_HERE"];
[Flurry setLogLevel:FlurryLogLevelAll];
...
}
```

Note that the `API_KEY_HERE` string should be your actual API key from when the app was first created, so feel free to copy that at this point.

There's also debugging information for you when you're first starting out (or any time, really). Ideally, you should disable this on release, but for now, it's helpful to see what's happening when testing.

Logging events

Events are the bread and butter of Flurry. They're essentially a limitless way of tracking your own custom events. Instead of keeping predefined functions or events, you have to simply pass the event name (simply a string) that you wish to track, and Flurry handles the rest for you.

As an example, let's say we want to track how many times our users start the game. Since we often visit the `MainScene`, we don't want a false positive being tracked. That being said, let's log the event only when they move a unit (but only on the first move, when `numTurnsSurvived` is equal to 1).

Open `MainScene.m`, and in the `moveUnit` function, add the following code to the top of the method that will log the `started_game` event for the current session:

```
if (numTurnSurvived == 1)
    [Flurry logEvent:@"started_game"];
```

Another example might be when a user finishes the tutorial. So in `MainScene.m`, in our `advanceTutorial` method, let's add an event for the case of our users finishing the tutorial:

```
- (void) advanceTutorial
{
    ...
    else
    {
        ...

        [Flurry logEvent:@"tutorial_finished"];
    }
}
```

And it's that easy to add event tracking! You can have an unlimited amount of differently named events, up to 300 unique events can be tracked per session (so make use of as many as you can that are relevant to your app/game), and there's no limit to how many times a given event can be tracked.

 There's also event logging with parameters, such as whether the user is registered or not, what device they're using, whether they're using a specific setting or not, and so on. Any string can be a parameter. You can read more about parameters within the Flurry API at `https://developer.yahoo.com/flurry/docs/analytics/gettingstarted/events/ios/`.

Flurry will automatically submit any session data when you're done using the app. Although that sounds rather ambiguous, it essentially sends data when the **Home** button is pressed.

That being said, if you're testing it, make sure your events are being logged correctly by Flurry using Xcode, and do not hit the **Stop** button before hitting the **Home** button on your device (or the simulator). The data may never be sent and you might spend hours or even days wondering why nothing seems to be working, when you actually never gave Flurry a chance to send the information.

Now that we have our events being logged and sent to the Flurry servers, let's actually track and analyze our data.

Tracking and visualizing the data

Thankfully, Flurry doesn't just grab our raw data, but actually creates useful analytics for us, so we don't have to do any analytics on the data ourselves. If you want to see, for example, how many people start a game every day, or how many people complete a game by surviving for more than 20 turns, you can easily see such data on their website. Here is a screenshot of what Flurry might look like after a few weeks of use:

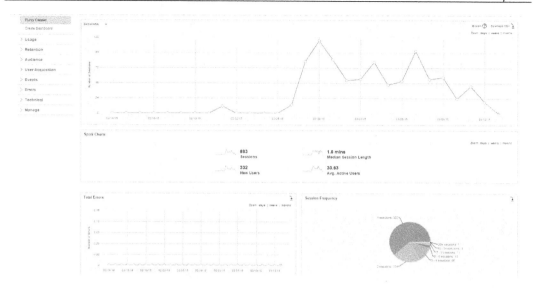

Note that it takes approximately 15 to 45 minutes for an event to appear in your Flurry event dashboard (not the data, but the event name). If, after a few hours, you're still not seeing the event listed in your dashboard, try again, but make sure you properly exit the app this time. This means pressing the **Home** button before stopping the app in Xcode so that Flurry can detect that event and send the data.

Also, Flurry isn't displayed in real time, so any actual data that gets sent to them is processed, and it may not appear for at least 24 hours. When testing, if you find yourself wondering where the data is, just wait for a day or two. Then it should start showing up. If it doesn't, make sure you're seeing the proper debug log messages in Xcode.

If you ever get lost using Flurry, want further explanation, or just want to know more about the advanced features of Flurry, you can look at their *Get Started* guide on their website at `https://developer.yahoo.com/flurry/#get-started`. It's fairly comprehensive.

If you're interested in alternatives to Flurry, you can look into iOS Analytics by doing a quick search, as well as by checking out `http://www.apptamin.com/blog/app-analytics-tools/`, which shows (and covers in detail) various other analytics tools.

Preparing the app on iTunes Connect

Now that we have everything ready, let's go ahead and get iTunes Connect (`https://itunesconnect.apple.com`) ready so that we can submit this game to be reviewed by Apple. This section assumes you already have a developer account and an app in iTunes Connect.

If you don't have a developer account, this is a good time to get it. If you're don't know how to get it, read *Chapter 1, Refreshing Our Cocos2d Knowledge*. If you do have a developer account, but haven't created the App in iTunes Connect yet, go back to the *Game Center* section of *Chapter 6, Tidying Up and Polishing*. There, you will see the step-by-step way to create an app in iTunes Connect. Once you've done that, you'll be ready to continue from here.

For the most part, iTunes Connect is fairly self-explanatory. However, we'll quickly see what each section is and what you need to enter.

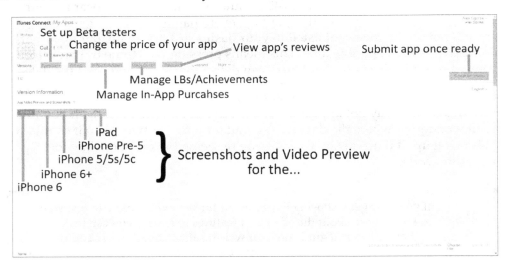

When you open your app in iTunes Connect, you'll see many sections at the top, as well as a section for the screenshots and the video preview. It's required that you include screenshots for every device you support. Since we're going to support all devices, it's best to add screenshots (and maybe a quick 30-second video) for each device.

Ideally, you should take your own screenshots for each device, which is why none are included in the project's files (maximum five screenshots per device can be added).

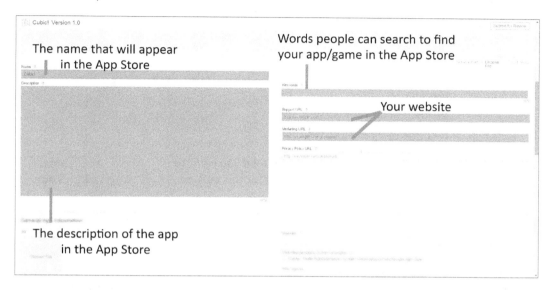

Below the screenshots, you'll see the app's display name in the App Store, a description (4,000-character limit) of the app that will be visible in the App Store, keywords that people can enter in order to find your app/game on the App Store, and a link to your website for users who want to learn more about you.

The keywords are comma delimited, and have a maximum of 100 characters. So, for example, the following are a few terms that could be used to describe this game. This string is 28 characters long:

```
cube,square,grid,number,math
```

If you need help determining the length of your keywords, you can just search for a string length counter, and generally, any one will do the job.

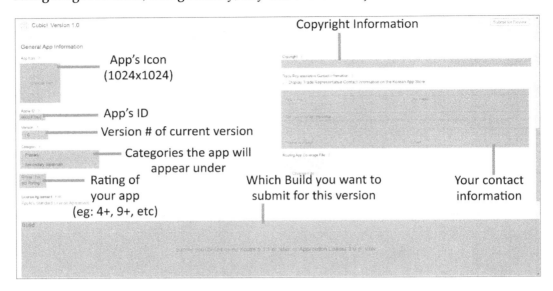

Next is the App's icon (this has to be 1024 x 1024, and in PNG or JPG format) — which will be displayed throughout the App Store — the version number, the categories it will appear under, and so on. An example of copyright information could be KeitGames 2015 (just imagine a little copyright symbol next to it when filling this part).

One thing to note is the **Ratings** section. Here, although it's subtle, you must click on the **Edit** button to go through the process of self-rating your app to determine what minimum age group the app is appropriate for. In our case, it's going to end up being 4+.

Also, after you submit a build to iTunes, it will go through a processing phase that lasts a few minutes. After that, in the **Builds** section, you can select which build you want to submit for the particular version of the app.

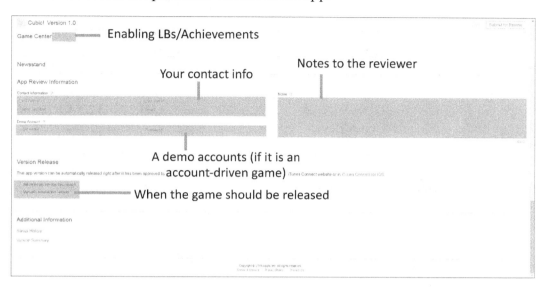

Next, we have the Game Center section. This is separate from the **Game Center** tab at the top of the screen because, even though you may have a working leaderboard set up and working within your test build, unless you enable **Game Center** here and select which leaderboard you want to add, it won't show up on the released version.

You can also provide a demo account if your app or game requires a login for it to work, as well as submit any notes you may have for the person reviewing your app.

Finally, If we select **Automatically release this version**, then whenever the app is approved by Apple, it will immediately begin processing for the App Store. It will then show up that day or the next (or whatever date in the future you have set in the **Pricing** section at the top). Suppose you choose **Manually release this version**. Then even if the app is approved by Apple, it will not begin processing (and thus will not be available for download, even after the set release date) until you click on **Release This Version**.

With all of the relevant information filled out, we can actually go through the process of creating a build and submitting it to Apple.

Releasing the game and steps after it

This is the part when the excitement really builds, and you say to yourself "It's time."

But seriously, it's an exciting moment when your game is finally ready for release and you're sending it to be reviewed by Apple with the plan that it gets into the hands of possibly millions of people.

The first thing to do when releasing a game is to create an archived file of your app that you can upload to the Apple servers. To do this, simply go to **Product** | **Archive** (if it's grayed out, change your device type from one of the simulators to a device, even if you don't have a device plugged in).

After the archiving is complete, a screen that looks like what is shown in the following screenshot will open (if it doesn't, you can go to **Window** | **Organizer**):

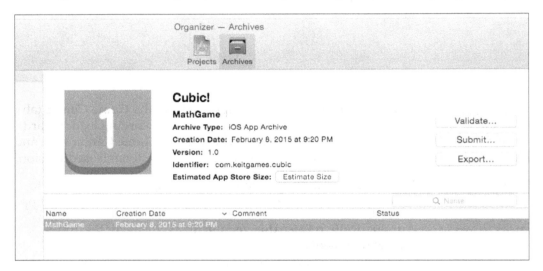

From here, click on **Export**. Choose **Save for iOS App Deployment** and click on **Next**.

Log in if you aren't logged in already, and it will take you to a screen that looks
something like this:

 If it says it can't find an app with a matching bundle ID, just click on **Try
Again**. It should find it the second time.

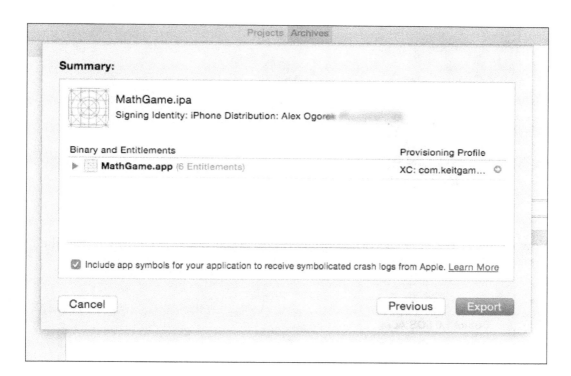

Click on **Export**, and then save it somewhere you can find later (such as the Desktop).

Now open the **Application Loader** by going to **Xcode | Open Developer Tool | Application Loader**. Sign in and choose **Deliver Your App**.

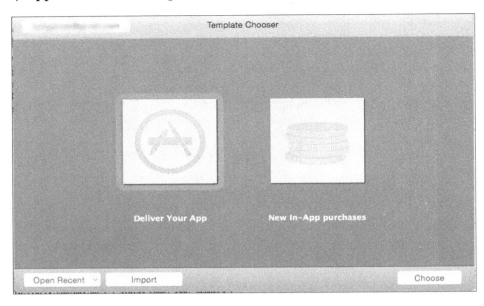

Now navigate to wherever you exported your IPA file, and open it. It will read the data, and the screen looks something like this:

When you click on **Next**, it will go through the process of verifying that all your icons are added properly and the default images exist, and anything else ensuring the app matches up with the information you provided.

If there are any errors, warnings, or issues that come up, chances are high that you're not the only person facing that issue. A quick Google search never hurt anyone.

Once the verification process is done, it will upload the app to Apple's servers.

 Note that this does not mean the app is "submitted" for review. It's just uploaded so that you can select it from iTunes Connect when you're ready. Even if it says something about being e-mailed when it's in review, that's not true (which is odd).

Now head back to iTunes Connect after waiting a few minutes, and you should see a **+** button next to the **Builds** section. When you click on it, you should be able to select the recently uploaded build.

Click on **Save** at the top. Then click on **Submit for Review**. Then complete the required questionnaire about what your app includes (in our case, none of them). Then click on **Submit**.

We're on our way!

 A faster way to validate and submit your apps to the App Store is without using the Application Loader. Instead of clicking on **Export**, you can click on either **Validate** or **Submit**, and the same process will take place.

After submission

Now that your app's status is **Waiting for Review**, it's best to make use of your time by either preparing for an update (because in theory, you could be constantly pushing updates, and as soon as one gets accepted, you push another) or marketing your game to the public.

Ideally, you've been doing all of this early on: blogging about your progress, posting about it on social media, telling your friends and family about the game you're creating, and so on. But if you haven't, no worries! The next few sections will guide you through this process.

Beta testers and the target market

If you don't have people playing your game and alpha or beta testing it yet, now's probably the best time to do it. You should try to get an array of players with different skill sets to see how different users interact with your game so that you can try to eliminate the confusion with as many people as possible.

Also, if you're wondering, "What kind of people should I look for to test my game?" you need to consider who your ideal player is. If you're making a kids' game, try to get kids (or maybe even their parents) to play your game. If the genre is tower defense, try to find people who just love tower defense games so that they can give you great feedback.

If you're interested in beta testing with people who aren't in your vicinity, consider Apple's TestFlight integration. At first, TestFlight was a standalone product, but now Apple has included it within iTunes Connect (you might have seen it if you went under the **Prerelease** tab). Essentially, you can invite people to use your app/game just by getting their e-mail. You upload a build in the same way you submitted it, except that you have to add the build to the prerelease, and after a review process, Apple allows the testers to download and play the game.

But having beta testers and figuring out your target audience is only step 1. Step 2 involves getting your game into the hands of many people.

App review sites

One of the keys to making your game a success is getting it into the hands of other people, especially people who write blogs or articles that are reviews of games other people have made. If a game is amazing, you'll see it all over the place, and maybe even Apple takes notice and features it under the **Featured** section of their App Store.

If you e-mail any developer (who isn't in a prominent company) and ask them how Apple featured them, the response is generally the same: "We had no idea that it was going to happen. We just asked some websites to review our game, and then all of a sudden, we were featured on the App Store for the week!"

That being said, there's a giant list of app review websites at `https://maniacdev.com/2012/05/ios-app-review-sites`, so that you don't have to find them yourself.

Although the URL says "2012," it has been updated as recently as August 2014, at the time of writing this book. The websites are sorted by Alexa ranking, which places the most viewed site at the top of the list (and the least viewed at the bottom).

Apple gives you 100 promo codes for every version you submit to the App Store. Use these codes when pitching/submitting your game to these sites.

 Note that it's not likely that your game will make it to a site like *Mashable* or *TechCrunch* right away without already being a big hit, so to make better use of the promo codes, it might be a better option to start lower on the list and work your way up, instead of down.

Other sources of information

There's a website known as *PixelProspector*. They have a ton of resources, links, guides, and more when it comes to game development (especially when it comes to indie games, which is most likely what you like if you're reading this book). Even if you're part of a reputed studio, this is still a great source for information (especially their relatively new **Marketing** section). Check it out at `http://www.pixelprospector.com/indie-resources/`. You'll probably find something useful.

Summary

In this chapter, you learned how to create a default image for your app, properly set up the icons (along with using the asset catalog), add analytics to your app via Flurry, set up everything on iTunes Connect, release your app, and plan what to do afterwards.

In the next chapter, we'll cover Apple's newest language, called **Swift**. We'll see a nongame example as well as a small game using Cocos2d's Swift version.

8
Exploring Swift

In the final chapter of this book, if your heart so desires, you can start learning Swift, Apple's new programming language. Here, you'll get a brief overview of what Swift is, how the language works, and some various syntax differences between Objective-C and Swift. We'll also cover the creation of a few simple apps using Swift.

In this chapter, we will cover the following topics:

- How Swift works
- Learning Swift through Playgrounds
- Using Cocos2d-Swift to create a game in Swift instead of Objective-C

This chapter will not cover most of Swift. It is instead intended as an introduction to coding in Swift through Cocos2d to create a game with this engine.

Also note that Swift, as a language, is only compatible with iOS 7 and above. If you intend to support iOS 6 or prior, you cannot use Swift in your project.

How Swift works

The main difference between Objective-C and Swift is in the way it looks. It still feels like Objective-C (in the sense that you can call all of the same methods), but the syntax is different.

For example, suppose you want to call this in Objective-C:

```
[object someMethodWithParam:param1 andOtherParam:param2];
```

Instead, you end up calling the following in Swift:

```
object.someMethodWithParam(param1, andOtherParam:param2)
```

Also, instead of using a header and a main file as in Objective-C, there's only a `.swift` file that gets used for everything.

There are obviously some syntax differences that you'll have to learn about when it comes to coding in Swift, but those who are familiar with Objective-C will pick up Swift quite easily. Don't worry, even if you aren't familiar with Objective-C. Swift is an easy-to-learn language, which makes picking it up much better.

That being said, let's cover some syntax differences using Apple's new tool they created to help learn and debug Swift—Playgrounds.

Learning Swift through Playgrounds

Playgrounds offer a way to test your Swift code quickly and easily without much baggage that usually comes when creating a test project in another language. They're intended as files used for prototyping and quick fiddling with code if you have problems with a small section. They're really easy to use and understand, so let's begin.

The first thing you'll notice about Swift is that there are no semicolons required (except when writing multiple statements on one line, which must be separated by semicolons). That's right—none! They're optional, but the preferred style of writing Swift code is without semicolons.

Also, when coding if statements, loops, switch statements, and so on, you must use curly braces around the block of code that will be run (even if there's only one line of code that will be executed).

Right now, go ahead and open the `SwiftSyntax.playground` file in the `Sample Projects` folder included with this book.

If you cannot open the file within Xcode, update your version of Xcode to the newest version, as your version might be outdated.

When you open this file in Xcode, you'll see a lot of things happening. It's separated via comment lines (// -----). Each section represents a different set of syntax differences between Objective-C and Swift.

Although it is not explicitly stated what the Objective-C equivalent is, you can see how to declare a variable, how to run loops, create and call functions, and so on. Also, not all the syntax differences with Swift are included here. Only the most common uses of the language appear here.

With the playground file opened, let's see how Playgrounds are organized so that you can better understand what's going on (and why Playgrounds are useful for purposes besides just being a place to hold code).

How Playgrounds are organized

The left side obviously has the code. The right side has a description of the state of the code; for example, if it's a variable, it will show the variable's value. If it's a `println` statement (the standard way to print the console in Swift), it will display the output.

If you type any new code in the Playground, you'll see the Playground's right-hand-side pane update as you type. If you copy and paste any code, you'll see all the lines updated with the final result of each line.

Because this is a Playground, we don't have to worry about using a `println` or `NSLog` statement here. It will automatically show up on the right-hand side of the Playground.

Viewing the results over time

One of the cool things about using Playgrounds is that you can track the progress of your loops over time. For example, if you want to see each item that was printed in the names array, or what the value of a variable is in each iteration, you can see it visually with the Playground's **Value History** button.

Also, if you want to debug your own Swift code in a project (and not just a Playground), you can bring it into a playground and observe the results over time. So if you have, say, an enemy patrolling back and forth with a loop, you can use the Playground's value history to see each value (in this case, position) at each iteration of the loop.

So first, go to the `for` loop section (approximately line 90), and find the line that says `total += x` within the `for` loop, as shown in the following screenshot:

```
87
88   //For syntax
89   var total = 0|
90   //up to but not including 100
91   for x in 0..<100 {
92       total += x
93   }
94   total
95
```

To view, move your mouse arrow onto the (100 times) line in the right-hand-side pane, and you should see two buttons appear on the right side of it. The first is an eyeball that will show you every value that a given object contains. For example, if you have a dictionary, you can view all the key/value pairs in that dictionary, as shown in this screenshot:

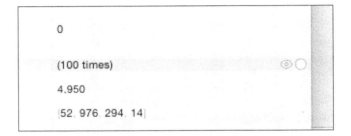

The second button is the **Value History** button. When your mouse arrow is on it, it will turn into a **+** button, as shown in the following screenshot:

When you click on this button, you'll see a chart showing the values of that variable over time as the loop iterates (you'll also see the output console, which displays the names being printed as expected, from the previous loop) as shown in this screenshot:

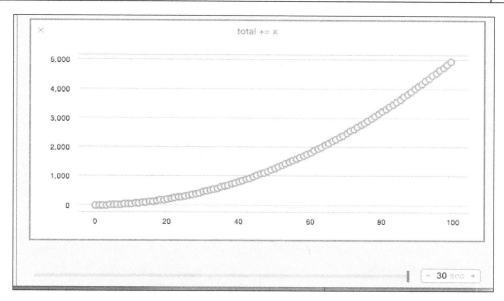

If you want to get more details of how your variable changes over time, you can either drag the red scrubber to the bottom of the **Value History** section, or click on any data point along the chart to see its respective value, as shown in the following screenshot:

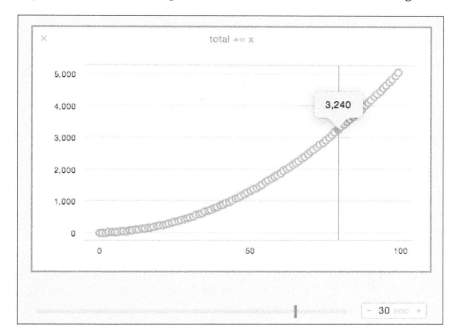

Learning more about Swift

There's a lot of content on Swift that wasn't covered here, such as lazy variables, the identity operator, the nil coalescing operator, class initializers, inheritance, and so on.

Some great places to learn more about Swift include `www.lynda.com` (a great course on Swift is at `www.lynda.com/Swift-tutorials/Swift-Essential-Training/180105-2.html`) and `www.raywenderlich.com/tutorials`, which have many online courses and tutorials that go over the basic and advanced features of Swift. You can also look at Apple's developer videos; just search for Swift at `https://developer.apple.com/videos/wwdc/2014/`. Then there are sample projects, the Swift developer blog at `https://developer.apple.com/swift/blog/`, as well as other websites such as Stack Overflow.

As mentioned earlier, Playgrounds can be very useful for developers who are just learning Swift, as well as those who are more experienced and wish to test their code for debugging purposes.

But a Playground isn't an app all by itself, so let's make a simple game using Swift as our language for Cocos2d. Again, you'll notice that the code itself is fairly similar to Objective-C; only the syntax is slightly different, so you should pick it up fairly quickly.

Creating a game in Swift instead of Objective-C

The idea behind using Cocos2d-Swift is to switch over to the new programming language, right? Even though the Swift version of Cocos2d is still relatively new, and everything might not be implemented by the time you read this book, it can still be used as the core language when creating a game. So let's make a very simple game here, building upon the core concepts you just learned and combining them with the knowledge you already have of how the Cocos2d engine works in general.

Why use Swift instead of Objective-C? Because, you should be staying up to date with the latest technologies in the field, and Swift is just the next step in that direction. Also, as the years pass by, Apple may slowly deprecate and stop supporting Objective-C (but that's just a theory).

In general, it helps to know more languages if the opportunity calls for it. And if you're interested in web development, Swift feels very similar to JavaScript, so it's like learning two languages at once.

So why Cocos2d-Swift specifically? For the same reasons you just read. Also, typing code in Swift is generally faster than in Objective-C, and so, if you can create code faster, you can, in theory, create games faster, which is awesome!

Goal of the game

The game we're going to make consists of a turret in the center that can shoot bullets, a score counter, and square-shaped enemies that come in from the left and the right. If the enemies make it to the center, it's game over! As the score increases, so will the spawn rate of enemies, eventually overwhelming the turret's fire rate.

Here are a few screenshots of the game we'll be making:

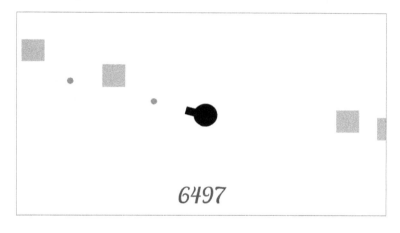

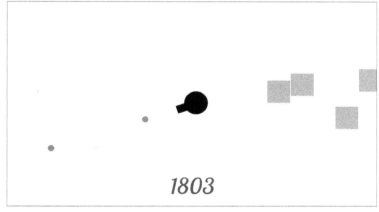

Starting a new Swift project

Remember, the way to start Cocos2d projects now is by going through SpriteBuilder. Even though we won't be using SpriteBuilder for any code, we still have to go through the process of creating a project there.

So, in SpriteBuilder, go to **File** | **New** | **Project**. Select the location where you want to create the project, name it something like `TurretGame`, and make sure you select **Swift** as the language. This is also shown in the following screenshot for your reference:

Then, in `Turret Game`, go to the `Assets` folder of this book's content, and drag the `Images` folder into the resources list on the left side of SpriteBuilder as shown in the following screenshot:

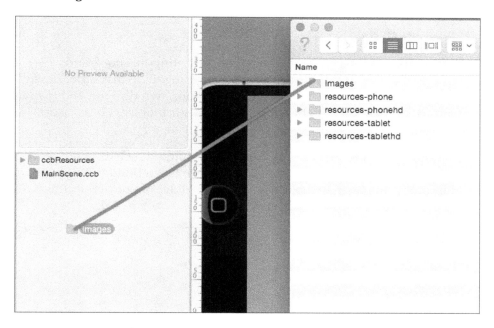

After it has been imported to SpriteBuilder, right-click (or press *Ctrl* and click) on the `Images` folder in SpriteBuilder, and select **Make Smart Sprite Sheet**. This is what TexturePacker normally does for us. However, we can speed up the process using SpriteBuilder's auto sheet maker, since this is only going to be an example project.

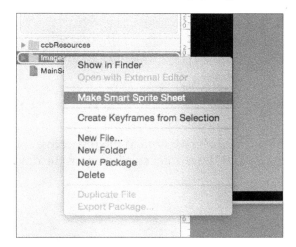

Once it has turned into a sprite sheet, the folder icon should be of a pinkish color with a smiley on it. Now, go to **File | Publish** so that SpriteBuilder can generate the necessary files for our project and we can be on our way.

Adding the font files

Unfortunately, SpriteBuilder is lame at the time of writing this book and doesn't handle BMFonts very well. So, what we're going to do instead of having SpriteBuilder handle the sizing/exporting is create our own BMFont and manually add it to our list of files. This might not be the most efficient way, but it works, so we're going with it.

In this book's project folder, you should see a list of folders such as `resources-hd` and so on next to the `Images` folder you dragged into SpriteBuilder. Copy all four of these folders and paste them in the iOS `Resources` folder of your project files. When it asks you, make sure you click on **Merge** (as well as **Apply to All**).

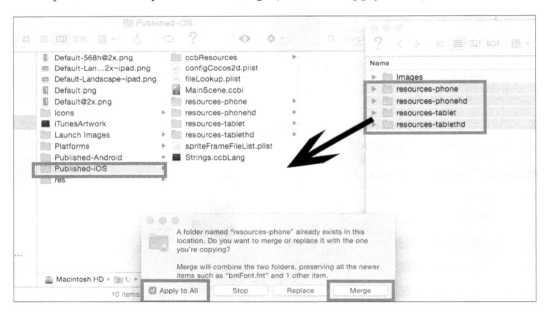

This will add the font files for each size type to the respective folder so that Cocos2d's directory search mode can find the correct size based on the device.

Importing Bridging-Header and loading MainScene

Objective-C, when working with Swift files, needs something called a `Bridging-Header` file. It's automatically created, so all we have to do is import the file. The format of the file is `ProjectName-Swift.h`, where `ProjectName` is the name of your project (for example, if the project is called `TurretGame`, we'll use `TurretGame-Swift.h`).

Now, feel free to open the Xcode project. Open `AppDelegate.m` and, at the top of the file, add the import statement to add the `Bridging-Header` file:

```
#import "TurretGame-Swift.h"
```

Then, in the `StartScene` method, we need to change the line of code that will transition to the main scene (as well as add a line that will read in our images sheet):

```
- (CCScene*) startScene
{
  // Capital "I"
  [[CCSpriteFrameCache sharedSpriteFrameCache] addSpriteFramesWithFile
:@"Images.plist"];
//[CCBReader loadAsScene:@"MainScene"];
  return [MainScene node];
}
```

We're using `node` here instead of `Scene` because we're calling a `Swift` class. In the previous examples in this book, the `Scene` method was a method we created, whereas `node` is a predefined function that does the same thing.

Creating the background, turret, and score label

Because Swift is intended to be short and to the point when it comes to readability, the following code is all that is required in the `MainScene.swift` file in order to get a white background, an image to display, and a label at the bottom of the screen (note the `CCScene` inheritance; the default is `CCNode`):

```
class MainScene: CCScene {

    let winSize = CCDirector.sharedDirector().viewSize()
    var background = CCNodeColor(color: CCColor.whiteColor())
```

```
     //a value of "527" to make sure it's working. It'll get auto-set
        later, don't worry.
     var lblScore = CCLabelBMFont(string: "527", fntFile:
        "bmFont.fnt")


     //"Images/turret.png" because the turret image was located
        inside the Images folder
     //also making sure to Downcast to a CCSprite from AnyObject!
  //We want to downcast because the variable we're setting should be
     a sprite, so because the spriteFrameByName() method returns
     AnyObject (as an explicitly unwrapped optional), we must
     downcast the ambiguous type to CCSprite for better use of the
     variable later on.
     var turret = CCSprite.spriteWithSpriteFrame
        (CCSpriteFrameCache.sharedSpriteFrameCache().spriteFrameByName
        ("Images/turret.png")) as CCSprite


  override init() {
     super.init()

     //simply add the background color
     self.addChild(background)

     //position and add the score label
     self.lblScore.position = ccp(self.winSize.width/2,
        self.winSize.height * 0.1)
     self.addChild(self.lblScore)

     //position and add the turret (z:1 so the bullets can spawn
        underneath it)
     self.turret.position = ccp(self.winSize.width/2,
        self.winSize.height/2)
     self.addChild(self.turret, z: 1)


  }
}
```

Run the project at this point, and you'll see exactly what we described as our result. If you're starting to appreciate how little code it takes to make stuff happen, then Swift just might be your language to learn.

Now let's move on to getting the turret to rotate.

Rotating the turret with touchMoved

Notice so far how just about all the classes and methods are named exactly the same, with minor syntax differences between Objective-C and Swift. It's going to be the same for our touchBegan, touchMoved, and touchEnded methods.

First, we need to add a variable to store the player's touch position. So, at the top of MainScene, add the following variable:

```
class MainScene: CCScene {
    ...
    var touchPos = ccp(0, 0)
    ...
}
```

Then, in the init() method, set the user interaction Boolean to true:

```
//records touches
self.userInteractionEnabled = true
```

Next, add the following methods to MainScene:

```
// a method that will be called when a touch is registered on the
  device

override func touchBegan(touch: CCTouch!, withEvent event:
  CCTouchEvent!) {
    // grab the touch's location within the scene, and set it
      to our variable
    self.touchPos = touch.locationInNode(self)
    // calculate the angle of the touch relative to the turret's
      current position
    var angle = ccpToAngle( ccpSub( self.touchPos,
      self.turret.position ) )
// set the rotation of the turret based on the calculated angle
  (converted to degrees because Cocos2D doesn't use radians)
    self.turret.rotation = CC_RADIANS_TO_DEGREES(Float(angle)) *
      -1
}

// a method called when a touch is dragged across the screen
override func touchMoved(touch: CCTouch!, withEvent event:
  CCTouchEvent!) {
// grab the location of the touch and set it again
    self.touchPos = touch.locationInNode(self)
```

```
        // calculate the angle again based on the new touch position
        var angle = ccpToAngle( ccpSub( self.touchPos,
          self.turret.position ) )
        // set the rotation of the turret again based on the new angle
        self.turret.rotation = CC_RADIANS_TO_DEGREES(Float(angle)) *
          -1
}

    override func touchEnded(touch: CCTouch!, withEvent event:
      CCTouchEvent!) {
        // do nothing at the moment
    }
```

If you run the game, you'll be able to drag your finger around and rotate the turret in the direction of your finger.

Shooting some bullets

Ours is not a very useful turret unless it's shooting bullets, so let's write that code.

First, we want a method we can call (or schedule). We want to make it spawn a bullet and then launch it in the direction of our finger (where the turret is pointing). So go ahead and add the following method:

```
func shootBullet() {

  //create the bullet. Again, "Images/bullet.png" because of the
    Images folder
    var bullet = CCSprite.spriteWithSpriteFrame
      (CCSpriteFrameCache.sharedSpriteFrameCache()
      .spriteFrameByName("Images/bullet.png")) as CCSprite

    //position the bullet underneath the turret
    bullet.position = ccp(self.winSize.width/2,
      self.winSize.height/2)

    //calculate the distance to move based on similar triangles
    let xDist = self.touchPos.x - self.turret.position.x;
    let yDist = self.touchPos.y - self.turret.position.y;
    let zDist = ccpDistance(self.touchPos, self.turret.position)

    let newX = (xDist * winSize.width) / zDist;
    let newY = (yDist * winSize.width) / zDist;
```

```
//assign that distance to a CGPoint variable
let moveDistance = ccp(newX, newY)

//create an action that will move the bullet, then after 0.5
    seconds, it will remove it from the screen
var moveAndRemoveAction = CCActionSequence.actionOne
    (CCActionMoveBy.actionWithDuration(0.5, position:
    moveDistance) as CCActionFiniteTime, two:
    CCActionCallBlock.actionWithBlock({

    self.removeChild(bullet)
}) as CCActionFiniteTime) as CCAction

//add the bullet
self.addChild(bullet)

//run the move action
bullet.runAction(moveAndRemoveAction)
}
```

Although we now have this function that will create a bullet and launch it along a path, we have no way of testing it yet. So, in our `touchBegan` method, we add a call to schedule the selector:

```
override func touchBegan(touch: CCTouch!, withEvent event:
    CCTouchEvent!) {
    ...
    //call it once, then schedule it
    shootBullet()
    self.schedule(Selector("shootBullet"), interval: 0.125)
}
```

Also, in our `touchEnded` method, we add a call to `unschedule` the selector (as we don't want the turret to shoot constantly):

```
override func touchEnded(touch: CCTouch!, withEvent event:
    CCTouchEvent!) {
    self.unschedule(Selector("shootBullet"))
}
```

If you're wondering why the selector is in quotes, let me tell you that that's just the syntax of Swift. Instead of explicitly stating the function, you have to pass the function name as a string, and Swift handles the rest.

If you run the game at this point, you'll watch those bullets go rocketing out of the turret when you drag your finger across the screen.

Spawning enemies and sending them towards the center

We want some enemies to shoot at, so let's create a method that will spawn an enemy along either the left or right wall, and send it to the center of the screen (where the turret is), over a period of 3 seconds:

```
func spawnEnemy() {
    //create the enemy. Again, "Images/enemy.png" because of the
      Images folder
    var enemy = CCSprite.spriteWithSpriteFrame
      (CCSpriteFrameCache.sharedSpriteFrameCache()
      .spriteFrameByName("Images/enemy.png")) as CCSprite

    //position the enemy randomly along the left or right wall
    let yPos = arc4random() % UInt32(winSize.height)
    let xPos = arc4random() % 2 == 0 ? -50 : winSize.width + 50
    enemy.position = ccp(CGFloat(xPos),CGFloat(yPos))

    //add the enemy to the screen
    self.addChild(enemy)

    //move to exactly 1 enemy-length away from the center
      (calculated with triangle ratios)
    let distanceToCenter = ccpDistance(self.turret.position,
      enemy.position)
    let xDistance = self.turret.position.x - xPos
    let yDistance = self.turret.position.y - CGFloat(yPos)

    let newDistanceToCenter = distanceToCenter - enemy
      .boundingBox().size.width
    let newX = (newDistanceToCenter * xDistance) /
      distanceToCenter
    let newY = (newDistanceToCenter * yDistance) /
      distanceToCenter

    let centerPosDistance = ccp(newX,newY)

    //create a move action that, after 3 seconds, will do
      something (nothing at the moment)
    let moveAndEndGameAction = CCActionSequence.actionOne
      (CCActionMoveBy.actionWithDuration(3, position:
      centerPosDistance) as CCActionFiniteTime, two:
      CCActionCallBlock.actionWithBlock({
      //do nothing at the moment
    }) as CCActionFiniteTime) as CCAction

    //run the move action
    enemy.runAction(moveAndEndGameAction)
}
```

It's great that we have a method to spawn enemies, but there are none currently spawning. So, just like the `shootBullet` function we scheduled, we must schedule the `spawnEnemy` function.

In the `init()` method, add the following line of code to spawn the enemies:

```
override init() {
    super.init()


    ...


    self.schedule(Selector("spawnEnemy"), interval: 0.35)
}
```

There we go! Now we have our enemies spawning. But even if they make it to their final position, nothing happens. Let's fix that.

Transitioning to GameOver

When an enemy gets near the center (after the action completes), we want our game to be over, so let's create a `GameOverScene` class, and transition to it when an enemy reaches their end position.

First, create a new file by hitting *Command + N* (or **File | New | File**). Select **Cocoa Touch Class** by navigating to **iOS | Source**.

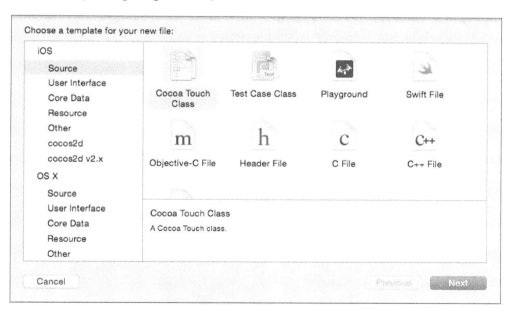

Then name it `GameOverScene`, and make sure you choose **Swift** as the language.

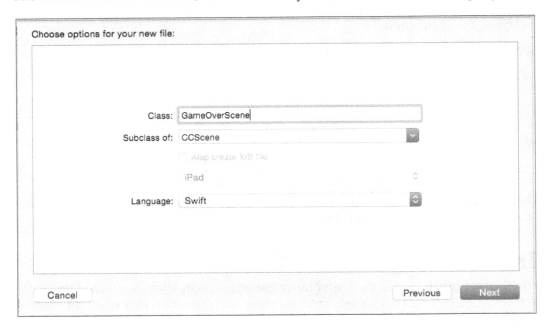

Save it in the `Source` folder of your project, and it will automatically open up.

Replace your `GameOverScene` class with the following, which will set the background to white, create a label in the center of the screen, enable touches, and transition back to `MainScene` when the screen is tapped:

```
class GameOverScene: CCScene {

  override init() {

    super.init()

    let winSize = CCDirector.sharedDirector().viewSize()

    var background = CCNodeColor(color: CCColor.whiteColor())
    self.addChild(background)

    var label = CCLabelBMFont(string: "Tap anywhere to restart",
      fntFile: "bmFont.fnt")
    label.position = ccp(winSize.width/2, winSize.height/2)
    self.addChild(label)
```

```
        self.userInteractionEnabled = true
    }


    override func touchBegan(touch: CCTouch!, withEvent event:
        CCTouchEvent!) {

        CCDirector.sharedDirector().replaceScene(MainScene.node() as
            CCScene)
    }
}
```

Then, to test this scene, add the following `replaceScene` call to the closure (or code block) of the enemy's move action in `MainScene.swift`:

```
func spawnEnemy() {
...
    //create a move action that, after 3 seconds, will do
        something (nothing at the moment)
    let moveAndEndGameAction = CCActionSequence.actionOne
        (CCActionMoveBy.actionWithDuration(3, position:
        centerPosDistance) as CCActionFiniteTime, two:
        CCActionCallBlock.actionWithBlock({

    //add this line - it will transition to the GameOverScene (in
        other words, the enemy was not killed)
    CCDirector.sharedDirector().replaceScene(GameOverScene.node()
        as CCScene)

}) as CCActionFiniteTime) as CCAction

    //run the move action
    enemy.runAction(moveAndEndGameAction)
}
```

Hmmm! Except now that it transitions properly, it's not much of a game, since we can't stop the enemies with the bullets we're shooting. Let's fix that!

Handling collisions

There's a ton of different ways to handle collisions, but the way we're going to handle them is by using the bounding box of our bullets and the enemies. To do that, we're going to set up two arrays (one for enemies and one for bullets) and a function to loop through the arrays and check for bounding box intersections.

First, we add two variables for the arrays. We're going to use `NSMutableArray` instead of Swift's arrays because Swift's array allows us to remove an item only via its index, and not by passing the item itself. So, it will be easier with `NSMutableArray`:

```
class MainScene: CCScene {

    . . .

    //arrays to hold our bullets and enemies
    var bullets : NSMutableArray = []
    var enemies : NSMutableArray = []

    override init() {
        . . .
```

Now we need to add our bullets and enemies to their respective array (as well as handle their removal from the array). So, in our `shootBullet` and `spawnEnemy` functions, we add the objects to the array, as well as remove the bullet from the array right before we remove it from the scene:

```
func shootBullet() {

    . . .

    var moveAndRemoveAction = CCActionSequence.
actionOne(CCActionMoveBy.actionWithDuration(0.5, position:
moveDistance) as CCActionFiniteTime, two: CCActionCallBlock.
actionWithBlock({

        //remove the bullet from the array
        //before removing it from the screen
        self.bullets.removeObject(bullet)
        self.removeChild(bullet)
    }) as CCActionFiniteTime) as CCAction

    //add the bullet
    self.bullets.addObject(bullet)
    self.addChild(bullet)

    . . .
}
```

```
func spawnEnemy() {
...


//add the enemy to the enemies array before adding it to the
  screen
    self.enemies.addObject(enemy)
//add the enemy to the screen
    self.addChild(enemy)


...
}
```

Next, we need to create a function that will loop through our arrays and check for collisions. If a collision is found, we will remove both objects from the arrays (and the screen) and break out of the loop so that we don't accidentally go out of bounds.

Create the following function in the MainScene.swift file:

```
func checkForCollisions() {

    //check for collisions
    for bullet in self.bullets {
      for enemy in self.enemies {

        //if the two bounding boxes are overlapping/intersecting/
colliding
        if CGRectIntersectsRect(bullet.boundingBox(),
        enemy.boundingBox()) {
          self.bullets.removeObject(bullet)
          self.enemies.removeObject(enemy)

          self.removeChild(bullet as CCSprite)
          self.removeChild(enemy as CCSprite)

          break;
        }
      }
    }
}
```

Finally, we need to schedule this function so that it will be called frequently enough when our bullets interact with the enemies, and the collision will get detected at the right time. To do that, simply schedule it in the `init()` function:

```
override init() {
    ...
    self.schedule(Selector("checkForCollisions"), interval:
       1.0/60.0)
}
```

Run the game at this point, and you'll see the bullets colliding properly. But no! It's not much of a game without a score counter. So let's add that to this example game in Swift.

Counting the score

All we need is a variable that tracks our score and a label to display it. Arguably, you can also have this on the game over scene, but we're not going to worry about that in this example.

So, at the top of our `MainScene` class, we create two variables as described, and then add the label to the screen in the `init()` method:

```
class MainScene: CCScene {

    ...
//a variable to hold the score. The value of 0.0 sets it to a
  Float type by default, not Int
  var score = 0.0
  override init() {
      ...
  }
}
```

Then we implement the `update` function, which gets automatically called by Cocos2d:

```
override func update(delta: CCTime) {
    //some obscure score increment over time...
    self.score += 0.47

    //set the label using String Interpolation
  self.lblScore.setString("\(Int(self.score))")
}
```

We also want to increase the score by `100` for every enemy that dies, so in the `checkForCollisions` function, we simply add `100` to the score variable:

```
func checkForCollisions() {
...
  if CGRectIntersectsRect(bullet.boundingBox(),
    enemy.boundingBox()) {
    ...
    self.score += 100
    break;
  }
}
```

If you run the game at this point, you'll see the score increasing as time goes on, as well as when any enemy gets hit by a bullet. The only thing left to do is make the game harder over time (because it's rather boring at the moment).

Increasing the difficulty

Finally (although it doesn't entirely matter for the purpose of making the example work), we want our difficulty to increase over time so that only the best players can make it far. We're going to do this by increasing the rate at which units spawn (every 2,000 points, to be exact). First, we want some variables to hold the current spawn rate as well as the amount of points accrued since the last increase in difficulty:

```
class MainScene: CCScene {
  ...
  //variables for enemy spawn rate (aka, difficulty)
  var spawnRate = 0.35
  var scoreSinceLastIncrease = 0.0

  override init() {
```

Then, we must replace the hardcoded value of `0.35` with the `spawnRate` variable:

```
override init() {
  ...
  self.schedule(Selector("spawnEnemy"), interval: self.spawnRate)
}
```

Now, every time we increase our `score` variable, we must also increase the `scoreSinceLastIncrease` variable. So in `update` as well as `checkForCollisions`, we need to add the same amount to both the variables:

```
func checkForCollisions() {
  ...
  if CGRectIntersectsRect(bullet.boundingBox(),
    enemy.boundingBox()) {
    ...
    self.score += 100
    self.scoreSinceLastIncrease += 100

    break;
  }
}

override func update(delta: CCTime) {
    //some random score increment over time...
    self.score += 0.47
    self.scoreSinceLastIncrease += 0.47

    //set the label using String Interpolation
    self.lblScore.setString("\(Int(self.score))")

}
```

Finally, we need to check inside our update: method whether the score since the last difficulty increase has crossed our limit (in this case, we're going to increase it after every 2,000 points earned). To do this, we'll just `unschedule` the `spawnEnemy` function, reduce `spawnRate` (only to a certain amount), and `re-schedule` the `spawnEnemy` function:

```
override func update(delta: CCTime) {
    ...
    if self.scoreSinceLastIncrease > 2000 {

      //unschedule and re-schedule the spawnEnemy method
      //using the new spawn rate
      self.unschedule(Selector("spawnEnemy"))

      spawnRate -= 0.025
      if (spawnRate < 0.005) {
```

```
        spawnRate = 0.005
    }

    self.schedule(Selector("spawnEnemy"), interval:
        self.spawnRate)

    //subtract 2000, the amount of the difficulty
    self.scoreSinceLastIncrease -= 2000
    }
}
```

Run the game at this point and watch as more and more units come flooding into the view, eventually overwhelming you.

And that's it! We've just made a very simple game in Cocos2d but with the help of Swift this time. It's not the best or most fun game in the world but it counts. Plus, this example was more of a way to show you how to go ahead and make games using Swift as your core language instead of Objective-C.

Summary

In this chapter, you learned how to make use of playgrounds and create a basic game using Cocos2d and Swift.

As mentioned earlier, if you wish to learn more about Swift, there's a plethora of available online resources at your disposal—online courses, Apple-created content, as well as online communities that provide assistance as needed.

Happy coding!

Index

Thank you for buying
Mastering Cocos2d Game Development

About Packt Publishing

Packt, pronounced 'packed', published its first book, *Mastering phpMyAdmin for Effective MySQL Management*, in April 2004, and subsequently continued to specialize in publishing highly focused books on specific technologies and solutions.

Our books and publications share the experiences of your fellow IT professionals in adapting and customizing today's systems, applications, and frameworks. Our solution-based books give you the knowledge and power to customize the software and technologies you're using to get the job done. Packt books are more specific and less general than the IT books you have seen in the past. Our unique business model allows us to bring you more focused information, giving you more of what you need to know, and less of what you don't.

Packt is a modern yet unique publishing company that focuses on producing quality, cutting-edge books for communities of developers, administrators, and newbies alike. For more information, please visit our website at www.packtpub.com.

About Packt Open Source

In 2010, Packt launched two new brands, Packt Open Source and Packt Enterprise, in order to continue its focus on specialization. This book is part of the Packt Open Source brand, home to books published on software built around open source licenses, and offering information to anybody from advanced developers to budding web designers. The Open Source brand also runs Packt's Open Source Royalty Scheme, by which Packt gives a royalty to each open source project about whose software a book is sold.

Writing for Packt

We welcome all inquiries from people who are interested in authoring. Book proposals should be sent to author@packtpub.com. If your book idea is still at an early stage and you would like to discuss it first before writing a formal book proposal, then please contact us; one of our commissioning editors will get in touch with you.

We're not just looking for published authors; if you have strong technical skills but no writing experience, our experienced editors can help you develop a writing career, or simply get some additional reward for your expertise.

Learning Cocos2d-x Game Development

ISBN: 978-1-78398-826-6   Paperback: 266 pages

Learn cross-platform game development
with Cocos2d-x

1. Create a Windows Store account and upload
   your game for distribution.

2. Develop a game using Cocos2d-x by going
   through each stage of game development
   process step by step.

Cocos2d-x Game Development Essentials

ISBN: 978-1-78398-786-3   Paperback: 136 pages

Create iOS and Android games from scratch
using Cocos2d-x

1. Create and run Cocos2d-x projects on iOS
   and Android platforms.

2. Find practical solutions to many real-world
   game development problems.

3. Learn the essentials of Cocos2d-x by writing
   code and following step-by-step instructions.

Please check **www.PacktPub.com** for information on our titles

Cocos2D Game Development Essentials

ISBN: 978-1-78439-032-7   Paperback: 136 pages

Bring your mobile game ideas to life with Cocos2D

1. Create interactive and fun gaming experiences using Cocos2D and Objective C.

2. Design impressive animations and import them into your game using SpriteBuilder.

3. Publish your games to iOS and Android using Apportable.

Cocos2d Game Development Blueprints

ISBN: 978-1-78398-788-7   Paperback: 440 pages

Design, develop, and create your own successful iOS games using the Cocos2d game engine

1. Enhance your game development skills by building different types of iOS games in Cocos2d.

2. Create games of many different genres using the powerful features of the Cocos2d framework.

3. A step-by-step guide with techniques to discover the potential of Cocos2d Game Engine with interesting projects.

Please check **www.PacktPub.com** for information on our titles

www.ingramcontent.com/pod-product-compliance
Lightning Source LLC
Chambersburg PA
CBHW060521060326
40690CB00017B/3345